DATE DUE

AP 15 '02			
MY 8 '02			
JE 5 '02			

The Wayward Preacher
in the Literature of
African American Women

For Monica, Renae,
Marjorie Charlotte, and Marjory May

The Wayward Preacher
in the Literature of
African American Women

by
James Robert Saunders

McFarland & Company, Inc., Publishers
Jefferson, North Carolina, and London

Excerpt from James Weldon Johnson's "The Creation" used with permission of Penguin USA. Excerpt from Paul Laurence Dunbar's "Little Brown Baby" used with permission of the University Press of Virginia.

British Library Cataloguing-in-Publication data are available

Library of Congress Cataloguing-in-Publication Data

Saunders, James Robert
    The wayward preacher in the literature of African American women /
by James Robert Saunders.
      p. cm.
    Includes bibliographical references and index. ∞
    ISBN 0-7864-0060-9 (lib. bdg. : 50# alk. paper)
    1. American fiction – Afro-American authors – History and criticism.
2. Clergy in literature. 3. Women and literature – United States –
History – 20th century. 4. American fiction – Women authors – History
and criticism. 5. American fiction – 20th century – History and
criticism. 6. Afro-American clergy in literature. 7. Afro-
Americans in literature. I. Title.
PS374.C55S28 1995
813.5'093522 – dc20   94-41242
                                                       CIP

McFarland & Company, Inc., Publishers
Box 611, Jefferson, North Carolina 28640

Table of Contents

Acknowledgments

I am grateful to Jerry W. Ward, Jr., of Tougaloo College who read the completed manuscript and rendered me a lengthy, encouraging response. I should mention that it was Jamie R. Barlowe at the University of Toledo who reminded me at a crucial juncture how important it is for a writer to be personally involved with his subject. I wish also to express my appreciation for Renae Shackelford-Saunders, also at the University of Toledo. The task has always fallen to her to tell me whether what I was doing was even worth the pencil and paper.

Preface

W.E.B. Du Bois, in his classic social treatise *The Souls of Black Folk* (1903), makes this assessment about the significance of the preacher in African American culture:

> The Preacher is the most unique personality developed by the Negro on American soil. A leader, a politician, an orator, a "boss," an intriguer, an idealist.... The combination of a certain adroitness with deep-seated earnestness, of tact with consummate ability, gave him his preeminence, and helps him maintain it [141].

Du Bois was intrigued by those preachers who flourished in the South during the period beginning just after slavery on through Reconstruction and up to the turn of the twentieth century. In the mind of Du Bois, an invaluable race leader himself, the preacher was a brilliant tactician who led the black race across treacherous terrain in the effort to gain ground following what must be regarded as one of the darkest chapters in our nation's history.

Indeed if we investigate the era of slavery itself, we find that the slave preacher was in a rather precarious position. Eugene Genovese, in his essay "Black Plantation Preachers in the Slave South" (1972), informs us that "slaveholders had, with reason, long distrusted black preachers as being too independent of spirit and therefore almost automatically a dangerous influence on the slaves" [193]. One has only to recall the prophet Moses demanding of old Pharaoh, "Let my people go," to appreciate the analogy that would be made several millennia later by black American

1

preachers who saw in the tormented Israelites a fitting symbol for what their own black congregations were undergoing. As those old-time preachers gave way to succeeding generations of exhorters, a tradition of leadership was maintained. The effort remained one of advancing the black community while simultaneously seeming not to want drastic change. Growing up in Richmond, Virginia, I would sometimes sit with my maternal grandmother, listening to her tell stories about the Reverend John Jasper, the former slave from Louisa County who traveled to Richmond after the Civil War and eventually became the renowned pastor of Sixth Mount Zion Baptist Church. That church was where my grandmother was baptized; Jasper himself did the honors. Much later, after my grandmother had died, I was ecstatic at discovering William Hatcher's biography, *John Jasper: The Unmatched Negro Philosopher and Preacher* (1908). Finding this work was a self-confirming experience for me as I began to attach new significance to my grandmother's early life.

I was no less excited with the publication of Raymond Gavins' *The Perils and Prospects of Southern Black Leadership: Gordon Blaine Hancock, 1884–1970* (1977), for the Reverend Hancock had been my own pastor when I was a boy. He lived on my block in Richmond, where within the black community, he was to become almost as legendary as Jasper had been. He espoused the doctrine of the "doubleduty dollar." Earn the dollar for subsistence, he encouraged his parishioners, and then buy goods and services from black entrepreneurs in order to keep the money in the black community. A theoretically valid economic plan that was made substantially less workable as integration opened up new markets to which blacks had hitherto been denied. But the church meant much more to me than just a source for economic proposals. In a manner of speaking, that church gave me life. From the Wednesday evening Boy Scout meetings to Sunday school classes, Vacation Bible School, and periodic Bible bees, I learned the essential lessons that enabled me to develop in a world that was often not receptive to little black boys.

How then, one might ask, could I stoop to desecrate that or any other church's memory? The answer in part has to do with the social assumptions supported by Du Bois as he unflinchingly accorded the preacher role to the male gender. It would perhaps be unfair to insist that Du Bois should have been any less chauvinistic than the times in which he lived. Still, chauvinistic and sexist are how those times must be defined. Anna Julia Cooper, in *A Voice from the South* (1892), reveals how even black institutions were discriminatory when it came to the issue of women and theology. All sorts of avenues were exploited by such institutions to insure that black women would be consistently left out. For so long in America, blacks have been regarded as a homogeneous group. And I am no less willing than others to entertain the prospect that once oppression has been leveled against an entire race, the first reaction should be for that race's members to hunker down and be supportive of one another against the frontal assault being waged by an oppressive white world. But how long should this unqualified hunkering down process go on? An important question, it seems to me, concerns what should be done when an element of the presumed homogeneous group itself takes on the form of an oppressor. A prime example is offered by the Senate confirmation hearings conducted in the fall of 1991 to decide on Clarence Thomas's fitness to hold a seat on the United States Supreme Court. In an eleventh hour move, Anita Hill came forward to accuse the nominee of sexual harassment. It is only on rare occasions that a black person is nominated to the highest court in the land. Should not the success of such a nomination be viewed as more important than a grievance based on circumstances purported to have occurred ten years earlier?

Gayle Pemberton characterizes what, for many, would be a heartrending dilemma:

> There are many hidden laws governing intraracial black behavior. One of the most important is the cardinal rule that says one simply does not complain about another black person to a white one, particularly a white person in a supervising position. A black woman *absolutely* does not indict a black man in front of a white one, as this act is hopelessly entangled within a welter of images and symbols from slavery [189].

The senators who conducted the Thomas hearings were examples of what Pemberton has in mind when she refers to white people in supervisory positions. The entire Senate panel was white; the two central people brought before them for interrogations were black, lawyers who had worked together as they negotiated their climbs up the ladder of success. There were those in the viewing audience who imagined that Hill and Thomas should have remained on the same side. The black race in this country is still involved in a struggle for equal rights. In the minds of some viewers, the point at which a black man was about to be appointed to the Supreme Court of the United States was not the time for a black woman to break ranks.

Yet breaking ranks is exactly what Hill did as she publicly accused Thomas of harassment. She was, as Nellie McKay explains, "a woman confronted with the difficult choice of telling or not telling the dirty details of what millions of women in this country suffer daily and are too afraid to dare tell" [277]. The telling was especially difficult for Hill because she knew what America's stereotypical perceptions were when it came to blacks and sexuality. Many whites still believe that blacks are promiscuous and inclined toward immoral sexual activity. The reality, however, is that harassment and other forms of abuse against women are a common phenomenon regardless of the racial factor. Some argue that Hill did the black race a disservice by testifying as she did at the hearings. But quite the contrary, by bringing her unfortunate experience to the nation's attention, she not only brought an important women's issue to the forefront, but she also made it possible to see the black race in a necessary new light. Instead of perceiving black women as mindless creatures unable to question the authority of black men, the country must now reassess the specific needs of black women and recalculate how the black race is merely a microcosm reflective of conditions that characterize the entire human race.

It is with this same general aim that the five black women authors I will be considering in this study undertook their portrayals of preachers. Long held up to be unassailable pillars of the community, these men of the cloth were not allowed to have human flaws. As right-hand men of God, they were expected to be the embodiment of perfection. They wore a mask that served an important function for their followers, a mask that most people would have been reluctant to see pulled down.

One of the striking things about Nella Larsen's *Quicksand*

(1928) is how tentative she is in her presentation of the possibility that the Reverend Pleasant Green is a philanderer. The most Larsen does, in this regard, is lay seeds for suggestion. After marrying Helga Crane, Pleasant "was, now, not so much at home . . . for the adoring women of his flock, noting how with increasing frequency their pastor's house went unswept and undusted . . . took pleasant pity on him and invited him often to tasty orderly meals, specially prepared for him" [151]. Helga is left to care for the children while Pleasant is free to pursue various activities, activities rendered vague in the novel but suggested, quite strongly, as one considers the very name of that preacher.

Zora Neale Hurston, in *Jonah's Gourd Vine* (1934), is more direct in characterizing the Reverend John Pearson as an adulterer. Since this novel is largely autobiographical, based on the lives of the author's own parents, there is the possibility that the writing of this work served as a catharsis. As a free-spirited girl growing up in the turn-of-the-century world of Eatonville, Florida, Hurston enjoyed secretly listening to men talking on the porch of Joe Clarke's grocery store. But that porch, where various forms of folklore were exchanged, was a world of men who held the power in town. Women were excluded and relegated to a position of lower status. John Pearson's behavior is a reflection of that patriarchal system. And yet, Hurston makes John a lovable character, as much the victim of social mores as he is also someone capable of taking advantage of the situation. He is what many women would regard as a bona fide "catch," a man at once handsome and possessed with high social status.

That is in fact how Etta Mae Johnson sees the Reverend Moreland Woods in Gloria Naylor's *The Women of Brewster Place* (1982). Having previously been relegated to a life without status or power, Etta can exult in the knowledge that "they'll be humming a different tune when I show up there the wife of a big preacher" [70]. While Moreland should be blamed for exploiting Etta's cravings for social status, Etta must share in the blame for her own victimization. In *Gourd Vine*, John's wife, Lucy, vows to her husband, "Ah'll never be 'ginst yuh." And this is after he has committed a multitude of transgressions against her and their marriage. Society in general though is also to blame because it has reinforced the notion that self-actualization on the part of

women can best be achieved when they enter into unions with
men who are upwardly mobile.

In Paule Marshall's *Brown Girl, Brownstones* (1959), we have
the concept of self-actualization presented from a different
perspective. Selina Boyce is the adolescent child of immigrant
parents who left their native Barbados in search of a better life
in America. For much of the novel, Selina identifies most with her
father, Deighton. While other parents tell their children what
they must do and become in this world, Selina declares with pride
that Deighton "never said I had to be anything." That guardian
symbolizes the universal need for individuality as he puts one plan
after another into motion in the effort to fulfill his identity.

After a tragic series of events, however, Deighton is driven
to seek solace in Father Peace's religious cult movement, and immediately we see individuality sacrificed at the altar of an organization that demands suppression of the self. We are reminded of
Ellison's *Invisible Man* (1952), where Brother Jack tells the atten-
tive narrator, "You mustn't waste your emotions on individuals,
they don't count" [284]. Marshall's Father Peace is a thinly veiled
version of Father Divine, who rose to prominence during the
Great Depression by offering communelike cooperatives and by
suggesting that indeed he was God. Without totally ignoring the
contribution that Divine may have made to the black community,
Marshall nevertheless points out with great clarity how religious
groups can be self-serving enterprises that thwart the attempt at
self-discovery.

Mildred Peacock, in Terry McMillan's *Mama* (1987), understands only too well how religion can be used as a tool to sway the
masses. The preacher this time is Mildred's own brother. He
postulates, "It seem like the harder you try, the less progress you
make" [176]. He lulls his listeners into virtual inaction, a state of
being that Mildred simply cannot accept. She is a single parent
with five children to raise; she must seek out ways to make sense
of the world on her own terms.

This brings us to the unavoidable issue of atheism. In *Quicksand*, Helga's bout with religion has left her so disenchanted that
she may indeed no longer believe in God. Larsen evidently wants
us to question the very existence of a supreme being, but each of
the other four authors affirms the notion that people should seek

interaction with the supernatural. What all the authors, including Larsen, are warning against is capitulation to religious functionaries who insist that the self must be virtually obliterated in order for salvation to be attained.

Note: Numerals inside square brackets [ ] in text and extracts refer to page numbers of the work being discussed.

NELLA LARSEN'S
Quicksand

The Attractive Trap: Helga Crane's Journey to Pleasant Green

When I was first introduced to Nella Larsen's *Quicksand* in the early 1970s as an undergraduate student, the professor's presentation of Larsen resembled Adelaide Hill's description of her in the 1971 edition. Hill maintained that Larsen "never found herself because she would not be White and could not be Black" [17]. In that "Harlem Renaissance" course, intriguing details of Larsen's life were discussed, including the fact that she was born to a West Indian father and a Danish mother and was caught in the paradoxical position of not having a firm grasp on her own identity while, on the other hand, functioning in the midst of a cultural movement that included the race-affirming works of W.E.B. Du Bois, Langston Hughes, and James Weldon Johnson. Her mixed ancestry was presented as a dilemma both for her and for us, as student investigators, while we sought to unravel the significance behind her presentation of *Quicksand*'s main protagonist, Helga Crane.

As the decades have passed, it has become clearer to me that Larsen's mixed ancestry was not as much the problem for academics and critics as the fact that here was a woman coming along in America during the 1920s who did not readily conform to the overriding social edicts. If mixed parentage had been such a tremendous spur to emotional crisis, then it certainly would have effected Du Bois with his French, New England Brahmin, and African heritage. He surely would have suffered an acute identity crisis. Similarly, James Weldon Johnson, whose father was a West Indian, would have had problems knowing who he was. Langston Hughes, raised without a father, would certainly have been in a quandary with regard to the Native American blood in his maternal grandmother, the woman who raised him for various lengthy intervals of his childhood. But in those instances, mixed heritage has not been the crucial factor in terms of defining who those writers were; it has not been raised as an issue to suggest that perhaps they were unsure of who they were within the context of the American racial spectrum. I would argue that in Larsen's case, as well, mixed heritage should not be offered as a means of presenting her as someone who was ambivalent with regard to her place within the racial spectrum.

Twenty years after I had enrolled in that "Harlem Renaissance" course, I was engaged in the process of selecting materials for my own "Harlem Renaissance" course and was astounded at how perspectives had changed with regard to Larsen. In his introduction to the 1992 edition of *Quicksand*, Charles Larson insists, "She did not pass for white after the decline of the New Negro" because "she was proud of her race and her own accomplishments" [xx]. She only published two novels, including *Passing* (1929), and it had been widely assumed that as the Great Depression phased out the "New Negro Movement" of the 1920s, Larsen retreated to the alternative pursued by many lighter-skinned blacks, that of passing for white to gain greater socioeconomic advantage. There is no evidence that Larsen "passed," only that she disappeared from the literary scene after writing that latter novel which many interpreted as the author's swan song and the biggest clue with regard to her subsequent intentions.

In his introduction to the 1971 edition of *Passing*, Hoyt Fuller professed that "Miss Larsen knew first hand the ambivalence of identity, and . . . she had gone off to Europe for a try at rejecting her Blackness" [12]. Actually, she sojourned in Europe during the early 1930s as the first black woman ever to receive a

Guggenheim Fellowship. Her intent was to write another novel, and if in doing so she encountered whites to whom she could in some ways relate, it should not be interpreted as a sloughing off of blackness, but instead as the investigation of a culture that was indeed a legitimate part of her parental background. That she chose Europe as the site for her Guggenheim endeavors should not be perceived any differently than if she had chosen Africa or the Caribbean.

Fuller presented this information with a noted bias, however, asserting that "Miss Larsen left her husband, Dr. Elmer Imes, and went off to live in Europe. Reportedly, she considered ending her marriage and becoming the wife of an Englishman. However, she finally returned to America and to Dr. Imes" [12]. Fuller would have served us better had he acknowledged that Imes was an incessant womanizer and that, in fact, years before she went to Europe, Larsen published two short stories in *Young's Magazine* ("The Wrong Man" in January 1926 and "Freedom" in April 1926) that were both centered around failed male/female relationships, both stories hinting at the tenuousness of her own marriage.

Larsen had married Elmer Imes in 1919 and by 1933 had obtained a divorce. The *Baltimore Afro-American* newspaper reported, as Larson indicated in his introduction, this chain of events with the same biased slant that Fuller would later use in his portrayal. The following are three headlines used by that newspaper to characterize the author's declining relationship with Imes:

> FRIENDS THINK LOVE COOLED
> WHILE WIFE WINTERED IN EUROPE
>
> FISK PROFESSOR IS DIVORCED BY
> N.Y. NOVELIST
>
> RECALL "JUMP" FROM WINDOW
> [xvi–xvii]

By the time they were married, Imes had been awarded a Ph.D. in Physics from the University of Michigan, a phenomenal achievement for a black man during the second decade of the twentieth century. It makes sense to conclude that Larsen was impressed with his credentials. As Thadious Davis reveals, she was not above being able to "inflate her educational background and previous employment, and emphasize that her husband had a Ph.D. in physics and worked *downtown* for an engineering firm" [250]. Larsen herself had no college credentials, but like many other blacks living in New York City at the time, she longed for the kind of fame that could come to her through association with the spawning New Negro Movement. Years before she would become a published novelist, she was a "mover and shaker" among notables in the Renaissance, largely because of whom she had married.

Although she struggled to save her marriage – she even joined Imes in Nashville when he received a professorship at Fisk University – his continuing philandering ways became more than she could bear, and on August 30, 1933, the divorce became final. Looking back at those *Afro-American* newspaper headlines, one becomes starkly aware of the prevailing social attitudes. It would seem that blacks steeped in a background of victimization, would have sought to avoid being victimizers themselves. Yet a "self"-victimization phenomenon took place in the black community. Themselves discriminated against as a race, black men proceeded with a program of discrimination against black women. For example, as Mary Helen Washington informs us in her introduction to *A Voice from the South*, there was a time when "no married woman – black or white – could continue to teach" [xxxii]. That custom was preserved by the male-dominated society as a whole, and even within the confines of a secluded black America, the standard was strictly maintained.

With that social reality as a backdrop, it becomes clearer why the headlines make Larsen's marital break-up seem entirely her fault. Nina Baym, in her essay "Melodramas of Beset Manhood" (1981), reminds us that "as late as 1977" the generally accepted American literary canon "did not include any women novelists" [123]. In particular, the black woman's place in the early 1930s was quintessentially in her man's home. This social perspective pervaded every corner of our society – education, business, and even the process by which texts were made available for casual reading. Baym notes that "the theories controlling our reading of American literature ... led to the exclusion of women authors from the canon" [123]. Of course, now with the advent of such black women writers as Toni Morrison, Alice Walker, and Terry McMillan, we need not be too worried about the prospect of black women ever being excluded again. But during the period in which Larsen wrote, women were not accorded their proper places at the heights of the literary ranks.

When Larsen's marriage disintegrated, it was, in the eyes of many, because she had not conformed to the behavioral patterns of a "respectable" wife. She was off writing novels, traveling to Europe on Guggenheims. She must have been crazy, and this time not merely because of her mixed heritage, but because she was busy writing novels when she should have instead been devoting her energies to preserving her marriage regardless of Imes's own marital shortcomings. No wonder she jumped from a window and broke her leg, as the *Afro-American* article under the headline "Recall 'Jump' from Window" attested. She was crazy. Never mind that Imes was having an affair with one of the members of Fisk's administrative staff right under his wife's nose for the entire university to see.

And then there is the novel itself – *Quicksand* – with its presentation of a woman who is in the beginning both single and employed but then, during the course of her many travels, winds up in a small town in Alabama, married to the Reverend Mr. Pleasant Green, who "consumed his food, even the softest varieties, audibly.... Though he did not work with his hands, not even in the garden, his fingernails were always rimmed with black.... He failed to wash his fat body, or to shift his clothing" [149]. He is not one of the more aesthetically pleasing characters in American literature, a factor made all the more obvious by virtue of the fact that his name is a blatant contradiction. Why would Larsen paint such a picture of a man, a man who fathers several children by his wife, Helga, and then, when she becomes too tired to keep up with all the housework, makes a beeline to "the adoring women of his flock," who "invited him often to tasty orderly meals, specially prepared for him, in their own clean houses" [151]? Pleasant leaves his family behind and goes off to feed his own belly, all the while admonishing Helga with such platitudes as "The Lord will look out for you," "We must accept what God sends," and "My mother had nine children and was thankful for every one" [151]. His mother may have been thankful for the miracle of her nine children's lives, but that does not mean she was not overburdened by work, a reality to which Pleasant might not have been privy. Or worse yet, a reality he has conveniently chosen to overlook as he attempts to convince Helga that her lot in life is to serve as his wife and to nurture however many children he wants. Immediately after the birth of her fourth child, Helga becomes critically ill. Although the illness is depicted as a physical one, it is more important to regard Helga's ailment as psychological, indeed spiritual. Her marriage to Pleasant and the subsequent bearing of children has left her feeling totally inadequate because she has not attained what she once perceived as necessary self-fulfillment. She evolves from the physical illness but has changed:

> During the long process of getting well ... Helga had had too much time to think. At first she had felt only an astonished anger at the quagmire in which she had engulfed herself. She had ruined her life. Made it impossible ever again to do the things that she wanted, have the things that she loved, mingle with the people she liked. She had, to put it as brutally as anyone could, been a fool. The damnedest kind of a fool. And she had paid for it. Enough. More than enough [159].

The tragedy of Helga's existence made it easy for the early critics to say that Larsen was suffering from an identity crisis that she presumably transferred to her main protagonist, who by this point in the novel is totally consumed in emotional turmoil. I would be remiss though if I did not also mention that not all of the early commentators were so critical of Helga's response to matrimony and childbearing. Hortense Thornton had suggested as early as 1973 that "when one considers the complex events of the novel, it becomes possible to argue that Helga's tragedy was perhaps more a result of sexism than of racism" [288]. So instead of characterizing Helga's, and thereby Larsen's, dilemma as one primarily involving race (which should she be, black or white?), one should analyze the extent to which Helga is the personification of the extreme difficulties that can accrue as independent-minded women pursue self-discovery in a male-dominated world.

Hugh Gloster, writing in 1948, summarily announced "because of her questionable background, Helga cannot integrate herself into either race" [143]. Two decades later the esteemed critic Robert Bone would likewise declare Helga "a neurotic young woman of mixed parentage, who is unable to make a satisfactory adjustment in either race" [102]. It was refreshing, indeed quite surprising, to find Larson espousing in 1992 an alternative view, one that Thornton must certainly appreciate. In his introduction, Larson asserts that "above all, hers is a portrait of loneliness and pain, despair and sorrow" [xiv]. What is most interesting, however, is that Larson specifies these elements as "qualities which bind her to the heroines of any number of later works by black women writers: Zora Neale Hurston, Ann Petry, Toni Morrison, Gayl Jones, Alice Walker, Gloria Naylor" [xiv]. Hurston's Janie Crawford, Petry's Lutie Johnson, Walker's Celie, and the women of Naylor's Brewster Place housing project all come to mind as Larson argues for Larsen being the precursor of the later feminist writers. This explains why so few could understand Larsen in her own lifetime (she died in 1964). The modern feminist movement with its accompanying group of feminist critics did not arise until the early 1970s. Can there be any doubt why a feminist-minded protagonist appearing during the 1920s would appear "neurotic" to a male scholar rendering pronouncements during the mid–1960s?

Hurston, in *Their Eyes Were Watching God* (1937), avoided the trap that Larsen's Helga fell into. Although she was married to Joe Starks for twenty years, Janie Crawford bore him no children. Prior to marrying Joe, she had been married to Logan Killicks. This first marriage produced no children either. By the time of her relationship with Tea Cake Woods, her biological clock may indeed have run out. But in any case, she would not have had children. Hurston was cognizant of the difficulties children can present, especially if one spouse desires to leave the other. The difficulty becomes exacerbated in distinct ways when the spouse who desires to leave is the woman. Helga contemplates leaving Pleasant but is tormented as a consequence:

> Of the children Helga tried not to think. She wanted not to leave them–if that were possible.... To leave them would be a tearing agony, a rending of deepest fibers. She felt that through all the rest of her lifetime she would be hearing their cry of "Mummy, Mummy, Mummy," through sleepless nights. No. She couldn't desert them [161].

It is not that women are more biologically equipped to raise children. Instead, it is a case of social dogma dictating women's roles. The dogma is so ingrained in the psyche of most people that while a man may desert his family and onlookers feel sad, if a woman deserts her children, we are thoroughly appalled and quite likely to detest her for doing such a horrible, unforgivable thing. How can a mother desert her own children? What kind of human being is she? These are the questions we would ask if Hurston's Janie and Logan had children. The couple do not have children, so we, unencumbered, can closely analyze the state of their marital relationship.

Already an old man at the point of his marriage to Janie, Logan is basically infatuated. As Janie confides to her grandmother, "He chops all de wood he think Ah wants and den he totes it inside de kitchin for me. Keeps both water buckets full" [40]. Perhaps Logan loved his new wife at one time. But something has changed and "Janie noticed that her husband had stopped talking in rhymes to her. He had ceased to wonder at her long black hair" [45]. The love or infatuation dwindles as his capacity to be oppressive increases. The husband now demands, "If Ah kin haul de wood heah and chop it fuh yuh, look lak you oughta be able tuh tote it inside. Mah fust wife never bothered me 'bout choppin' no wood nohow" [45]. One can safely conclude that if Logan ever was in love with Janie, he has fallen out of love and the relationship will eventually deteriorate to the point where he will not even mind if she works herself to death. He will buy a second mule so that she can help him plow the fields. Whatever happens to her will just happen; he no longer cares. As readers, we can be happy that she deserts him while he is off making the purchase that would have further tied her to him and the land he owns, upon which she stood to be little more than a common day-laborer.

We are reminded of Helga's Pleasant as Janie is describing Logan to her grandmother:

> His belly is too big . . . and his toe-nails look lak mule foots. And 'tain't nothin' in de way of him washin' his feet every evenin' before he comes tuh bed. 'Tain't nothin' tuh hinder him 'cause Ah places de water for him. Ah'd ruther be shot wid tacks than tuh turn over in de bed and stir up de air whilst he is in dere. He don't even never mention nothin' pretty [42].

Both men are fat, either their toenails or their fingernails are dirty, and, to be blunt, they simply stink.

Janie, as a girl, envisioned her life as a tree about to bloom. Her life might well have contained all the beauty of a flower. Helga had wanted "to do the things that she wanted, have the things that she loved" [159]. Like Janie, she had wanted her life to be sheer possibility, a wonderful adventure in development. But such was not to be the case with Helga, for hardly had she recovered from the severe illness accompanying her fourth pregnancy (this child dies at the age of one week), than "she began to have her fifth child" [162]. These are the words that end the novel. Considering the images of entrapment and suffocation that increase as the novel winds to its conclusion, and considering the symbolic portent of her serious illness both during and after the fourth pregnancy, it is not inconceivable that this fifth pregnancy will spell her demise, if not in the physical sense, then surely in the sense that spiritual death is inevitable.

What drives Helga to Pleasant Green in the first place? The novel begins with her as a twenty-two-year-old teacher at a "school for Negroes" in the deep South. Her craving to do meaningful, unusual things is evident even then. She has an "urge for beauty, which had helped to bring her into disfavor in Naxos" [41]. She dresses in vivid colors and makes no bones about her desire to obtain and enjoy the finer things of life. But the school is oppressive, weeding out those who refuse to accept its rigid doctrines. "Teachers as well as students were subjected to the paring process, for it tolerated no innovations, no individualism. Ideas it rejected, and looked with open hostility on one and all who had the temerity to offer a suggestion or ever so mildly express a disapproval" [39]. Nevertheless, Helga maintains her individuality, vowing to resign, leave Naxos, and end her engagement to James Vayle, a member of the town's black upper crust.

Helga confronts Dr. Anderson, the principal, and tells him how much she hates the institution as she rattles off a checklist of flaws. "I hate hypocrisy," she insists. "I hate cruelty to students, and to teachers who can't fight back. I hate backbiting, and sneaking, and petty jealousy" [53]. This is one of the first images in the novel of an encroaching suffocation. The lack of freedom to think for oneself amounts to a type of imprisonment, so Helga is preserving herself when she stands firm in the resolve to leave as soon as possible. Anderson is momentarily disarming, entreating Helga, "What we need is more people like you, people with a sense of values, and proportion. . . . You musn't desert us, Miss Crane" [54]. In some ways he sounds like a politician, spouting off phrases such as "a sense of values and proportion" and "we need . . . more people like you." It is certainly not how most bosses would react to a worker who had just told them how much she hated the job.

We must also keep in mind the nature of the times during which Anderson lives and functions as the administrator of this Negro school. It is near the turn of the century, one or two generations after slavery. Negro schools are in a precarious situation in the deep South. Many whites are opposed to racial uplift and will do anything to deter the process of educational advancement. Many blacks are suffering from low self-esteem and cannot believe that they will one day, through their descendants, achieve equal rights in this land where slavery was once an ongoing enterprise. These are the odds that Anderson is up against in his position as the administrator of this all-black institution. He can ill afford to make any mistakes, so closely is he being watched.

It furthermore follows that Anderson has to be careful how he might express any affection for a female member of his staff. Even in more contemporary times, some organizations will not allow husbands and wives to work together, and these same organizations will discourage intimacy between staff members. Thornton would have us consider that "Dr. Anderson is perhaps the only male character who accepts Helga's individuality" [296]. As I mentioned earlier, he does not respond to her complaints as the average supervisor might. It is very possible that he is smitten by her. And he does have some appreciation for her as a unique human being. He takes a risk in confirming her basic grievance as he lectures her:

> Someday you'll learn that lies, injustice, and hypocrisy are a part of every ordinary community. Most people achieve a sort of protective immunity, a kind of callousness, toward them. If they didn't, they couldn't endure. I think there's less of these evils here than in most places, but because we're trying to do such a big thing, to aim so high, the ugly things show more, they irk some of us more [53–54].

The principal seems concerned about Helga's development, but he may be going to the lengths that he does out of self-interest. Although it is true that "lies, injustice, and hypocrisy are a part of every ordinary community" [53–54], how could he know "there's less of these evils here than in most places" [54]? Rather than an expressed concern for accuracy, his words might best be understood as a reflection of his desire for her to stay because of romantic inclinations on his part.

Romantically inclined or not, alarms should be going off for us when we hear the language Larsen uses to describe Anderson's attempts to keep Helga on the payroll. "He had won her" [54], the narrator says. It is as though Helga had been an inanimate prize or, even worse, a slave purchased at an auction block. When Anderson tells her, "You have dignity and breeding" [54], though he may have thought he was giving her a compliment, he causes her great inner turmoil. She is not one of society's blue bloods. Indeed, the whole notion of social breeding only reminds us yet again of the "peculiar institution" under whose auspices black women and men were mated for the express purpose of proliferating various slave types.

In analyzing Anderson, it is also important to remember that he is responsible for the visit of the "holy white man" who at the campus chapel "had spoken of contentment, embellishing his words with scriptural quotations and pointing out to them that it was their duty to be satisfied in the estate to which they had been called, hewers of wood and drawers of water" [37]. Harriet Jacobs, in her slave narrative, *Incidents in the Life of a Slave Girl* (1861), renders the white Reverend Mr. Pike, who is but an earlier version of Larsen's white preacher. Urging slaves to accept their lot in life, Pike admonishes, "Servants, be obedient to them that are your masters according to the flesh, with fear and trembling, in singleness of your heart, as unto Christ" [70]. Both preachers, especially the latter, take their texts from Colossians 3:22–24, where the apostle Paul stipulates: "Servants, obey in all things your masters. . . . And whatsoever ye do, do it heartily, as to the Lord. . . . Knowing that of the Lord ye shall receive the reward of the inheritance." Paul advises slaves to be happy with their lot. But one thing Paul does, that these more modern-day preachers do not do, is admit his shortcomings. A book earlier, in Philippians

3:12–14, the apostle perceives the perfection of Christ and acknowledges, "Not as though I had already attained. . . . Brethren,
I count not myself to have apprehended: but this one thing I
do. . . . I press toward the mark for the prize of the high calling
of God." Paul, even while he writes, acknowledges his imperfections as he seeks moral betterment through the ideals of Christ.

William Herzog maintains, "Paul knew how incomplete his
resocialization in Christ had been, and he had few illusions about
the character of Christian life as moving from struggle unto
struggle, not victory unto victory" [215]. Paul wrote his epistles
from a jail cell, not for personal gain or blind adherence to the
status quo, but because he sought closeness to God. Paul's inability
1900 years ago, during the time of the Roman Empire, to con-
ceive of a society without slaves should not be attributed so much
to personal inadequacies as it should be attributed to an old-world
view of things that had not yet been sufficiently splintered by
alternative approaches to how people should live.

We must consider whether or not that excuse can continue to
hold up by the year 1845. Frederick Douglass was one who did not
think so. In his narrative published that year, he bluntly states:
"I am filled with unutterable loathing when I contemplate the
religious pomp and show, together with the horrible inconsis-
tencies, which every where surround me. We have men-stealers
for ministers, women-whippers for missionaries, and cradle-
plunderers for church members" [120–21]. Slavery at any point in
history, in any realm, must be regarded as wrong. And 1900 years
ago, across various sections of the world, men were stolen,
women were whipped, and babies were sold away from their
families into slavery. But Douglass is appalled at the open hypocrisy of church affiliates being so deeply involved in the perpetuation of so many human atrocities. Nineteen hundred years ago
might have been too early for the initiation of widespread change
with regard to this matter. But a century and a half ago was late
enough in time for whites in the ministry to know, with a certain
clarity, the difference between right and wrong.

The white preacher in *Quicksand* can likewise be held accountable in much the same way that the white school official Ed-
ward Donleavy in Maya Angelou's autobiographical *I Know Why
the Caged Bird Sings* (1970) must be held accountable for the

differentiation in types of equipment being processed for the Negro school and the white school. Whites will have access to microscopes and other chemistry equipment, while blacks will receive "some new equipment for the home economics building and the workshop" [153]. Donleavy's intention is for blacks to function only in service occupations and be relegated to the lower levels of that Southern social strata. The place is Stamps, Arkansas, in the early 1940s. Donleavy loves the way things are done there just as Larsen's white preacher loves Naxos "because Naxos Negroes . . . knew enough to stay in their places" [37]. This is the world that Anderson has helped perpetuate. And in the final analysis, Helga comprehends some of what lurks behind his message and she recovers enough to reconfirm her previous commitment to leave the school.

Helga understands that she will not be able to fulfill herself in a place like Naxos. It is not clear whether she has surmised that Anderson might have ulterior romantic motives. But one senses, at this point, that even if his intentions are along those lines, she would not be interested. She is young, her whole life is before her, and her instinct toward self-discovery will not even allow her to entertain serious notions of settling down. Helga is engaged to James Vayle, who "was liked and approved of in Naxos" [42], but once she has decided to leave, she acknowledges that "even had she remained in Naxos, she would never have been married to him" [57]. He is just another socially accepted fixture she endures as a condition of her brief Naxos tenure. Their sexual relationship has not been consummated. The most "she had allowed him" were "frequent kisses under the shelter of some low-hanging willows" [58].

Critic Deborah McDowell, remarking on the then prevailing social code, asserts that "the only condition under which sexuality is not shameless is if it finds sanction in marriage" [151]. Women who engaged in premarital sex or extramarital sex were regarded as whores, parasites living on borrowed time compared to members of the more virtuous society. Even in accepting James's kisses, Helga is uncomfortable, concluding that "she must have been mad" [58]. Yet, she is unclear whether she has violated any personal ideals. She thinks, during those interludes of foreplay, that she has gone mad, "but she couldn't tell why she thought so"

[58]. It bothers her that she has been forced to be so out of touch with her own feelings. But such is the standard for Naxos, just another reason why Helga has determined to try her lot elsewhere.

Unfortunately, however, life does not get easier upon Helga's arrival in Chicago. In preparing to search for a job, "she dressed herself carefully, in the plainest garments she possessed, a suit of fine blue twill faultlessly tailored, from whose left pocket peeped a gay kerchief, an unadorned, heavy silk blouse, a small, smart, fawn-colored hat, and slim brown oxfords" [63]. She has thus compromised her position, because she once felt that "bright colors were fitting." Still, work will be difficult to come by. She tries the local library and various employment agencies, but discovers that references are needed, something she will not be able to obtain because she left the Naxos Negro school in the middle of the school year. Desperation sets in as Helga undergoes

> days of this sort of thing. Weeks of it. And of the futile scanning and answering of newspaper advertisements. She traversed acres of streets, but it seemed that in that whole energetic place nobody wanted her services. At least not the kind that she offered. A few men, both white and black, offered her money, but the price of the money was too dear. . . . She began to feel terrified and lost [66].

Even as early as the 1920s, Chicago was a bustling city with its share of menial opportunities for minorities. Helga's difficulty finding employment has a lot to do with the fact that she is a single woman with no one to vouch for her. She is alone, not a state of being that society has yet sanctified as an acceptable condition for a young attractive woman. She must have a place, belong to someone, or she will be regarded as strange.

This notion of woman as object for possession becomes amplified with the occurrence of men offering money for sexual services. As conservatively dressed as she is, why would men assume she is a prostitute? Larsen with the subtle rendering of this situation is suggesting that regardless of the attire, there are those men who view women only in terms of their availability to afford men pleasure. Further, the universality of this perspective is conveyed through the remark that black as well as white men perceive Helga this way. Helga's response is quite appropriate. She feels like a lost lamb in the wilderness, where wolves are ever-present. One cannot blame her for being terrified.

Helga has become a "lost child" of the sort that black women leaders such as Mary McLeod Bethune were interested in at the turn of the century. Bethune started her institute for girls at Daytona Beach, Florida, in 1904, and she became president of Bethune-Cookman College during the 1920s when her institute merged with another in the interests of racial advancement. Bethune was the leading black woman figure of her time, and it is highly probable that Larsen used her as a model for her character Mrs. Hayes-Rore in order to expose additional details about how society viewed independent women. Described as "a prominent 'race' woman," Mrs. Hayes-Rore gives Helga a job without requiring any references, presumably because, as that benefactor herself abruptly states, "I'm interested in girls." No longer married, Hayes-Rore has for some time been alone, married to her social mission that is, in fact, helping girls to get along in the world. But society will have its doubts concerning exactly what Hayes-Rore's "interests" in girls are, just as it always has had certain prurient questions about females' relationships with one another.

Just as society has been quick to stereotype women who are intimately involved with and devoted to others of their sex, society has also stereotyped women as being intellectually inferior to men. So when a woman like Bethune rises from being the daughter of former slaves to being an adviser to the president of the United States, she still is mainly seen, by the world at large, as a woman subject to the same sexist evaluation process that other women have undergone. Regardless of how effective Bethune may have been, many still regard her as a physically ugly woman who pandered her services to the highest political bidder. And despite how much she accomplished in the field of education, there are those who argue she did not accomplish as much as certain of her contemporaries such as Booker T. Washington and W.E.B. Du Bois. Hayes-Rore is described as a "woman with badly straightened hair and dirty fingernails" who steals "ideas, phrases, and even whole sentences" from "Frederick Douglass, Booker T. Washington, and other doctors of the race's ills" [70]. She appears as someone who, try as she might, will never rise to the status of the men she presumably is trying to emulate.

Helga travels with Hayes-Rore to New York City as her assistant. It is there that our young protagonist meets her benefactor's niece-in-law, Anne Grey, "a person of distinction, financially independent, well connected and much sought after" [76]. Anne owns her own home, has an "impeccably fastidious taste in clothes," and is "almost too good to be true ... almost perfect" [76]. However, the operative word there is "almost." While Anne may appear to be almost perfect, Helga will ascertain within this person a significant measure of hypocrisy. Anne claims to hate whites but imitates their style of dress and manners. She proclaims the greatness of black culture but detests "the songs, the dances, and the softly blurred speech of the race" [80]. It is that hypocrisy, in part, that drives Helga to leave New York and investigate the homeland of her mother as a possible place where she can feel comfortable and continue her development.

But Copenhagen, Denmark, proves not to be the refuge that Helga had hoped. Her relatives, the Dahls, are mesmerized by her, yet they are in awe of her because she is black. Aunt Katrina insists, "You must have bright things to set off the color of your lovely brown skin. Striking things, exotic things" [98]. Uncle Poul regards Helga with a similar fascination. In fact, many in the town of Copenhagen stop to stare at "the queer dark creature." Helga comes to feel that she is on exhibition, like a "pet dog" of the sort that had never been seen before. She is viewed as exotic, "almost savage," something not altogether human.

In such a world, one might imagine that a person who is an artist would be able to empathize with Helga's situation. Artists, being outsiders themselves, should understand the plight of others who have somehow been made to feel different. Larsen, in this work, presents her version of the eccentric artist through the character of Axel Olsen, who is "a tallish man with a flying mane of reddish-blond hair. He was wearing a great black cape, which swung gracefully from his huge shoulders, and in his long, nervous hand he held a wide soft hat" [101]. With his "broad streaming tie," he stands out as someone ostensibly not part of the herd. And thereby, Larsen makes her point all the better, for Olsen will show himself to be not very much unlike many other men. He propositions Helga, and when she refuses his offer for an "informal arrangement," he resolves that in order to have Helga he must marry her. Because he holds a position of high social status, he assumes that her answer will be yes, and in prematurely accepting his "prize," he reveals an unattractive aspect of himself. In what amounts to an acceptance speech, Axel tells Helga, "You have the warm impulsive nature of the women of Africa, but, my lovely, you have, I fear, the soul of a prostitute. You sell yourself to the highest buyer. I should of course be happy that it is I" [117]. Conceding to the social stereotypes of his day, he confirms our suspicions that he is just another person who regards women as objects that are available for a man to possess.

Helga is adroit as she insists, "I'm not for sale. Not to you. Not to any white man. I don't at all care to be owned. Even by you" [117]. She is emphatic in her assertion that she "couldn't marry a white man." But is this really the reason why she will not marry Axel? Hortense Thornton believes we should "question the extent to which her acknowledgement of race is used as a mask for her sexual repression" [299]. Perhaps Helga's rejection of Axel has nothing to do with the fact that he is white. In her meditative essay "Coming Apart" (1980), Alice Walker makes an interesting observation as she uncovers "the roots of vicious white male pornographic treatment of white women" [41]. Walker would have us reevaluate the institution of slavery, not just as it existed in the United States, but as it has existed throughout history all the way back to ancient times. Slave women have served as a "pornographic outlet." Slavemasters, of whatever hue, had license to use slave women for both pleasure and profit. Helga seeks a break in the perpetuation of that cycle. She will not have sex without being married. An illicit sexual relationship is, in her mind, unacceptable. But just as Helga never could have married James Vayle, she cannot marry Axel because she is astute enough to recognize that even sex within the boundaries of marriage will pose certain limitations to which she will not accede.

We admire Helga for once again having avoided the trap, a trap made all the more obvious when she views Axel's portrait of her. "Collectors, artists, and critics had been unanimous in their praise and it had been hung on the line at an annual exhibition" [119]. Those collectors, artists, and critics are a microcosm of the world at large which perceives women from particular stereotypical perspectives. Helga, on the other hand, condemns that portrait as being "some disgusting sensual creature with her features" [119]. The portrait is a distorted rendering of the subject, not "herself at all," but a sexually provocative image that is as much due to the vision society in general holds of women as to Axel's adherence to the standard.

Although Helga insists that she is returning to America to attend the wedding of Anne and Dr. Anderson, Helga's former principal, we can safely assume that she has grown weary of Copenhagen's social mores. Even Aunt Katrina and Uncle Poul's marriage has its inadequacies. They have stayed together mainly for "security, balance." What becomes apparent, however, at this point is that Helga has begun to go in circles. She is returning to New York and, in fact, to Anderson, who can mean nothing but disaster for her now since he will be a married man, and married, no less, to the woman she once regarded as her best friend. When she was previously in New York, living with Anne, she had run into him at "a health meeting," one of Harlem's uplift activities. It was Anne who had informed her that "he had been too liberal, too lenient, for education as it was inflicted in Naxos" [84]. The suggestion is that he had been fired or perhaps more delicately separated from involvement with the work of that school. The hint we got when he was principal – that he represented something other than the status quo – takes on added significance as we now can conclude he has the tendency to be a maverick.

Ann Hostetler, emphasizing the factor of sexuality in the novel, contends that "for Helga, Anderson seems to represent creative potential . . . the possibility that she can reconcile her sexuality with her identity as a black American woman" [43]. But Hostetler also acknowledges a danger that Helga herself has perceived. Anderson comes across at that health meeting as someone not quite sure how he will approach Helga, and she "was conscious of the man's steady gaze. The prominent gray eyes were fixed upon her, studying her, appraising her" [81]. It is difficult to ascertain the significance of the fact that he is staring at her, but Larsen certainly has not carelessly and coincidently used the word "appraising." Appraising as one would evaluate a rare jewel, an object, a possession. Helga, even at this point, has a deep emotional attachment to Anderson. "She was aware too," Larsen tells us, "of a strange ill-defined emotion, a vague yearning rising within her" [82]. We could call it love, but when he visits her, days later, she seems totally ambivalent about their relationship. Larsen has rendered expertly the picture of a tormented soul, for "until the very moment of his entrance she had had no intention of running away, but something, some imp of contumacy, drove her from his presence, though she longed to stay" [82]. Again, Larsen has chosen her words carefully – an "imp of contumacy." Helga continues to stubbornly resist what she resisted when she and Anderson were in Naxos. She rejects the emotional liaison. Anderson himself detects she is "still seeking," eager to fulfill that identity Hostetler had noted as being so important.

A great tragedy becomes evident as we witness how Helga has, in effect, thrown Anderson back to be taken by Anne. While our heroine may want to be independent, we have to be concerned about the psychological detriment that sexual repression causes. However heroic, it must be assumed that at a certain point, pent-up sexuality will burst forth in a flood. After Anderson has married Anne, Helga literally bumps into him at a party, where in a secluded moment:

> He stooped and kissed her, a long kiss, holding her close. She fought against him with all her might. Then, strangely, all power seemed to ebb away, and a long-hidden, half-understood desire welled up in her with the suddenness of a dream. Helga Crane's own arms went up about the man's neck [133].

Hostetler is very critical of Anderson's action; she condemns him for responding "to Helga according to the cultural stereotype of women as objects of desire" [43]. But we should also consider what Thornton has to say about the incident. The latter critic notes a development in Helga, who "assumes a new role of aggressor, or manipulator of events" [299]. We do not know exactly what to make of the fact that Helga, as a guest at yet another party, has "had to go upstairs to pin up a place in the hem of her dress which had caught on a sharp chair corner" [133]. She fixes the hem and steps, still secluded, out into the hall but "never quite knew exactly just how" she wound up in the arms of Anderson. He may indeed experience, as Hostetler puts it, "a dark, primitive sexual attraction" to Helga, but Helga herself seems to be just as culpable in the ultimate outcome of that encounter. She has indeed reached the point of desperation in her willingness to have an affair with this now married man, and when he later defends himself as having been too drunk to know what he was doing, it is all she can do to hold herself together.

It is in this turbulent emotional state that Helga first encounters Pleasant. Unable to remain in her hotel room, she "tore open drawers and closets, trying desperately to take some interest in the selection of her apparel" [138]. She dresses in her normal style with colors that others of her generation would have regarded as too flamboyant. Although it is pouring rain, she wanders out into the street, propelled by a stiff wind that "whipped cruelly about her." Tired and weak, she makes her way into what Larsen at first refers to only as a "store." Helga has no idea what building she has entered and knows only that she has gained a reprieve from the inclement weather. Only after she hears the singing of spirituals does she realize she has wandered into a storefront church in which she finds herself seated with a woman pressed against her on one side and a "fattish yellow man" on the other. This man is none other than Pleasant, who has traveled up from Alabama for reasons that we are never told.

When another female member of the congregation shrieks, "A scarlet 'oman. Come to Jesus, you pore los' Jezebel" [141], it becomes obvious that this entire small gathering thinks Helga is a prostitute who has come in from the street seeking to repent. Helga must wriggle out of her wet coat in order to free herself from the woman's grasp. Meanwhile, "at the sight of the bare arms and neck growing out of the clinging red dress, a shudder shook" Pleasant who is still sitting to the protagonist's immediate right [141]. Is he appalled at her because he regards her dress as being inappropriate? Remember, she is soaking wet. When she was not noticing, he had cast "furtive glances" at her between his shouts of "Amen!" and "Praise God for a sinner!" Larsen goes to great lengths to make Pleasant's motives unclear. He could be shuddering because he is appalled at the soaking wet tightness of her dress or he could be shuddering as a consequence of being sexually attracted to her. His "furtive" glances might be the surreptitious quick looks of a shy man or of a man aware that he, as a minister, is not supposed to be examining women in the congregation. The woman next to Helga shouts, "Glory! Hallelujah!" because a soul is about to be saved. Pleasant shouts, "Praise God for a sinner!" and we are not exactly sure why he is glad that the "sinner" has arrived.

When Helga leaves the worship hall and is on her way back to her hotel, Pleasant's intentions become at least a bit clearer. He offers to escort her back to her room, and during their walk she is "obliged to lay firm hold on his arm to keep herself from falling" [143]. Thornton believes that Helga here becomes the manipulator of events. In an epiphany-like revelation, the protagonist realizes that

> the man beside her had himself swayed slightly at their close encounter.... She cast at the man a speculative glance, aware that for a tiny space she had looked into his mind, a mind striving to be calm. A mind that was certain that it was secure because it was concerned only with things of the soul, spiritual things, which to him meant religious things. But actually a mind . . . consumed by some longing for the ecstasy that might lurk behind the gleam of her cheek, the flying wave of her hair, the pressure of her slim fingers on his heavy arm [143].

Helga's own mind "had become in a moment quite clear." But this momentary vision she has of Pleasant fades quickly back into ambiguity. It is as though they are both in the process of repressing their natural instincts, Pleasant having to do so because of his ministerial position, Helga because of her Victorian notions of how a woman is supposed to behave.

What is it specifically that attracts Pleasant to Helga? We know that she is what is commonly referred to as a "mulatto," a person having one parent black and the other white. American literary history is replete with examples of how this condition can be quite tragic. Authors as diverse as Langston Hughes (in his play *Mulatto*, 1935) and William Faulkner (in his novel *Light in August*, 1932) have investigated the plights of these outsiders who belong to neither one race nor the other. In explaining, though, the specific attraction that Helga holds for Pleasant, it is useful to consider Charles Stember's provocative chapter "The Sexual Preferences of Minority Males," where he stipulates that the "black internalization of white criteria of beauty is deeply rooted and pervasive, having originated in precolonial times and continuing to receive reinforcement both from the white society and from the black family itself to whom the value of a Caucasian appearance was manifest in society" [90–91]. It is not difficult to understand how American slaves could have regarded themselves as inferior in every sense from intellect to physical appearance. It was reflective of the general psychological damage done by that peculiar institution. The unfortunate corollary, however, is that decades after slavery had ended, many blacks continued to adhere to the very standards that had been previously enforced to their psychological detriment.

I would argue, in addition, that a lustful nature of the sort that operates in most males is a factor in Pleasant's sudden fondness for Helga. This is not to say that lust manifests itself whenever any man encounters any woman. As a rule, men are much more selective than that. Furthermore, not every man is attracted to women. But I am speaking in general terms about an aspect of manhood that Ralph Ellison was seeking to convey through his careful juxtapositioning of Jim Trueblood with Mr. Norton. Trueblood hypothesizes, "Maybe sometimes a man can look at a little ole pigtail gal and see him a whore" [59]. What is of particular interest in this case is what Trueblood, the incestuous black sharecropper, has in common with the wealthy white philanthropist Norton. On the one hand, they represent divergent social entities. But on the other hand, they are very much alike in their pathological sexual inclinations. On reconsidering *Quicksand*, we can similarly conclude how much alike the diverse characters Anderson, Axel, and Pleasant are in terms of how they perceive Helga.

It just so happens that by the time Helga meets Pleasant she has grown weary of rebelling against social dictum. Larsen is subtle. That night at the hotel Helga "pressed her fingers" into Pleasant's arms (note that it is no longer just one arm) until a "wild look" came into his eyes. That is how one paragraph ends. The succeeding paragraph begins with "the next morning," and we are told that Helga is reviewing "the happenings" of the previous night. She could have been reviewing events that occurred at the storefront church, or perhaps she was pondering her walk home with Pleasant and the reciprocal emotions evidenced during that phase of their encounter. Or perhaps the relationship was consummated through sexual intercourse, and in reviewing the previous night's happenings, she is contemplating the chain of events that led to her loss of virginity.

In what amounts to one of the quickest courtships in literary history, Helga is married to Pleasant, presumably on the same day of her contemplations, and travels with him to "the tiny Alabama town where he was pastor to a scattered and primitive flock" [146]. Having been "saved," she is now desirous of making a contribution, bringing enlightenment to that rural community. Robert Fleming, in his essential essay "The Influence of *Main Street* on Nella Larsen's *Quicksand*" (1985), draws distinct connections between these two works. Sinclair Lewis was raised in a place similar to the small town of Gopher Prairie where the major action of his novel is set, so he understood well what life was like in such a closed and inhibited society. Even before arriving at Gopher Prairie, Carol Kennicott yearns to "get my hands on one of these prairie towns and make it beautiful. Be an inspiration" [11]. But both Carol and Helga meet with obstacles that will make their yearnings difficult to put into effect.

Carol wants to "teach the lambs" a more sophisticated culture, but she learns that "the lambs were wolves" much more interested in gossiping and other trivial pursuits. Gopher Prairie natives think Carol believes she is better than them. Whenever she proposes a project, they are eager to see her fail. Helga is unable to pursue her vision (for a more enlightened community) due to a different reason. Within a period of twenty months, she has three children and these "children used her up." Suddenly "there was no time for the pursuit of beauty, or for the uplifting of other harassed and teeming women, or for the instruction of their neglected children" [150]. We see a woman struggling for mere survival, going through cycles of "sinking into chairs" and waiting for the "horrible nausea" to pass. Ironically, there are "adoring women" in Pleasant's congregation who stand by, as Helga becomes increasingly weary, to fix him "tasty orderly meals." The "wolves" in *Quicksand* are all too eager now to look down on Helga, who becomes so sick during and after her fourth pregnancy that she ceases to function at all.

After having spent several years in Gopher Prairie, Carol wonders out loud to Guy Pollock, the town lawyer who has some semblance of a free spirit:

We're all in it, ten million women, young married women with good
prosperous husbands, and business women in linen collars, and grand-
mothers that gad out to teas, and wives of underpaid miners, and farm-
wives who really like to make butter and go to church. What is it we
want – and need? Will Kennicott there would say that we need lots of
children. ... But it isn't that. There's the same discontent in women
with eight children and one more coming – always one more coming!
And you find it in stenographers and wives who scrub, just as much as
in girl college-graduates who wonder how they can escape their kind
parents. What do we want? [197]

Through Carol, Lewis has raised an important social question:
What do women want from their lives? Granted, no two women
are alike and accordingly no two women will want the exact same
things. Indeed, many women are perfectly satisfied being "good"
wives and "good" mothers. But Larsen wants us to be critical of
the smugness with which Pleasant tells the toil-weary Helga, "My
mother had nine children and was thankful for every one." We
have to be skeptical when a man defines what makes a woman
satisfied. We also have to consider the period during which Pleasant's mother lived and raised her children, a time just after
slavery when, needless to say, many black women would have
been ecstatic at the prospect of raising children outside the bonds
of white ownership. Carol Kennicott answers her own question
with regard to what women want by asserting, "We want everything." The stage is thereby set for an increasingly progressive
society where there can be no sex-based limitations.

Carol tells Guy: "We're tired of drudging and sleeping and dying. We're tired of seeing just a few people able to be individual-
ists" [197]. Lewis's protagonist is in a sense speaking for all
humankind, both women and men, when she comments on how
only a very few have access to ultimate social freedom. We are
all bound by institutions, supervisors, mores, mandated sched-
ules. Few of us indeed are free to control the boundaries within
which our lives are forced to fit, boundaries which nevertheless
have for generations been more facilitative of the endeavors of
men.

Much has been made of the *Haustafeln* (Household Duties)
passages in the Bible: Colossians 3:18–4:1 and Ephesians 5:21–
6:9. Colossians 3:18 and Ephesians 5:22 read identically, man-
dating, "Wives, submit yourselves unto your own husbands." To

a large extent, the tradition of family has evolved from those passages, with men the acknowledged heads of their respective households. On numerous occasions I have been told by members of the clergy that women should find a way to submit regardless of the types of husbands they have. Furthermore, they should not opt for the convenient escape of divorce. This, some ministers will maintain, is a major reason why there is a breakdown in the nation's social fabric, particularly as pertains to the family.

What those ministers emphasize less is the mutuality aspect of the Haustafeln. Paul, in Colossians, also urges, "Husbands, love your wives" (3:19). In Ephesians, he explains, "So ought men to love their wives as their own bodies" (5:28), and he stipulates, "Husbands, love your wives, even as Christ also loved the church (5:25). If we cannot be certain that a man cares enough about himself so that caring similarly for his wife will amount to an abundance of love, we can at least be sure that the notion of Christ's love for the church is indicative of extreme self-sacrifice. So even as Paul tells wives to obey their husbands, he sets key conditions. He does not tell women to stay with their husbands regardless of how the men treat them. One can be rather certain that the apostle would not, for example, have ordered a woman to remain with a physically abusive husband until she was beaten to death.

The question now, with regard to Pleasant, becomes one of determining whether or not psychological abuse is much better. Simone de Beauvoir, in her treatise *The Second Sex* (1953), relates an anecdotal tale that is at once reality and symbolic horror. She recalls seeing

> in a primitive village of Tunisia a subterranean cavern in which four women were squatting: the old one-eyed and toothless wife, her face horribly devastated, was cooking dough on a small brazier in the midst of an acrid smoke; two wives somewhat younger, but almost as disfigured, were lulling children in their arms. . . . As I left this gloomy cave . . . in the corridor leading upward toward the light of day I passed the male, dressed in white, well groomed, smiling, sunny. He was returning from the marketplace, where he had discussed world affairs with other men; he would pass some hours in this retreat of his at the heart of the vast universe to which he belonged, from which he was not separated. For the withered old women, for the young wife doomed to the same rapid decay, there was no universe other than the smoky cave, whence they emerged only at night, silent and veiled [77–78].

Much like de Beauvoir, Hurston has a way of conveying reality through metaphor. De Beauvoir has used a cave (the realm of women) and juxtaposed it with the entire universe (the realm of men). In the very first paragraph of *Their Eyes*, Hurston provides us with a metaphorical ocean where the dreams of men are drifting on distant waves: "For some they come in with the tide. For others they sail forever on the horizon, never out of sight" [9]. The point being made, of course, is that for men, big dreams are at least possible. Even if their wishes are not fulfilled, they are "never out of sight." They can dream with a much higher degree of probability that their dreams will come true, if not for them, then perhaps for their sons.

In the name of woman, Carol Kennicott proclaims, "We want everything." Considering that acknowledgment, it is perhaps significant that Carol winds up having only two children spaced reasonably apart. Her domestic duties will not be as overwhelming as Helga's. But we get a clear sense of what some in the Gopher Prairie community have in mind for women when Sam Clark offers the explication: "Carrie Kennicott's a smart woman, and these smart educated women all get funny ideas, but they get over 'em after they've had three or four kids. You'll see her settled down ... behaving herself, and not trying to butt into business and politics" [428]. Lewis was writing *Main Street* while the battle for women's suffrage in America was still being waged. Needless to say, many men and women still felt that politics (and even business) was not the proper realm for women. What is amazing is that over the decades large segments of the world's population have not altered their sexist attitudes. They believe a woman's place is still in the home and any divergence from this approach to life is seen as a serious social detriment.

Buchi Emecheta, in her ironically titled book *The Joys of Motherhood* (1979), presents us with a character, Nnu Ego, who is possessed with a strong individualistic spirit. Her last name signifies that very fact. Yet, as she is expecting her sixth child, "it occurred to Nnu Ego that she was a prisoner, imprisoned by her love for her children. ... It was not fair, she felt, the way men cleverly used a woman's sense of responsibility to actually enslave her" [137]. Nnu continues having children, nine in all, but as we reach the closing pages of that novel we find an embittered woman who tragically feels that she has not made the best use of her life. It is easy to say, well, the children make up for it, she should take solace in having brought into the world and nurtured so many other lives. There are in fact those who abhor birth control and abortion for that reason. But we must consider who, in the first place, makes the laws concerning women's bodies. What social ends are being served? Nnu concludes her best interests are not made a priority in the process. Of her husband, she asserts, "He owns me, just like God in the sky owns us" [217]. Sexist perspectives have relegated women to a social position where male domination, however subtle, is nonetheless ever present. In the marital union, the act of having children is quite often only a further means of entrapment.

This is the "quagmire" Helga feels "ruined her life" and "made it impossible ever again to do the things that she wanted, have the things that she loved, mingle with the people she liked" [159]. She has become one of the inhabitants of de Beauvoir's cave, which is not unlike the cave of Carol Kennicott's fable, where there is "a cavewoman complaining to her mate. She doesn't like one single thing; she hates the damp cave, the rats running over her bare legs, the stiff skin garments, the eating of half-raw meat, her husband's bushy face" [276]. Carol's cave, like de Beauvoir's, will serve better for our analyses if we look at its symbolic portent. The rats, stiff garments, and half-raw meat allude to the misery many women feel at being bound to the walls of their homes. The torture is so great for Helga that she is relieved when her fourth child dies shortly after birth.

How can all this tragedy be going on around Pleasant and he not be aware of it? I would argue that he has been so severely blinded by what he has taken to be the biblically ordained roles of men, as differentiated from women, that he cannot see his wife's pain. Or worse, he does not care because in the submissive role in which she has been cast, her yearning for a full life is not as important as his undertakings, especially since he perceives himself as an agent of God Almighty. This husband is adept at spouting off high-sounding phrases such as "the Lord be praised" and "trust the Lord more fully, Helga." But he has not taken the time to learn who she really is. He had not perceived, or cared an awful lot, that she had pursued him from the very first, on that rainy night in New York, in order to escape from the restrictions of an outside sexist world. She submitted to marriage as the only logical alternative to her problem of a stunted identity. "And anyway there was God," she had rationalized. She saw herself as getting two chances in one, reaching out, as she was, like a person sinking fast in quicksand, grasping for branches that turn out to be only thin air.

Had he been truly concerned about her salvation, this man of the cloth could have turned to other biblical passages besides the Haustafeln that he seems to rely on. He might have looked to Galatians 3:28, for example, where Paul asserts, "There is neither Jew nor Greek, there is neither bond nor free, there is neither male nor female: for ye are all one in Christ Jesus." The implication there is that in the eyes of God, we are all equal regardless of socioeconomic status, race, or gender. Or instead of focusing on Ephesians 5:22 – "Wives, submit yourselves unto your own husbands" – which by itself can be terribly misleading, he could have jumped back one verse to Ephesians 5:21, where the mutuality factor is expressed as profoundly as anywhere else in the Bible. That verse does not just say that wives should submit to husbands who love them supremely. It calls for an equal "submitting yourselves one to another in the fear of God." We need only look at the relationships that Jesus had with women, relationships that Katharine Sakenfeld calls "exceptional and even revolutionary," to know that He desired individuals to gain fulfillment through a personal commitment to spiritual development. It is what Janie, in Hurston's novel, finally realizes when she tells Pheoby Watson: "Two things everybody's got tuh do fuh theyselves. They got tuh go tuh God, and they got tuh find out about livin' fuh theyselves" [285]. Certainly, an intermediary of Pleasant's limited caliber is not fit for the task at hand.

Annis Pratt informs us that "in the woman's *bildungsroman* tension between the hero's desires and society's dictates results in archetypal narrative patterns of pursuit and submission, accompanied by images of suffocation, dwarfing, and mental illness" [41]. That archetype would apply four-square to Helga's predicament except that this heroine's illness toward the end of the novel is physical instead of mental. Larsen leaves Helga's thought processes intact because it is through Helga and her decline that we understand the flaws of religion as practiced by those who are either blatant hypocrites or basically ignorant of the very text they claim as the guide for their lives. Helga is losing faith in the very existence of a supreme being, "for had she not called in her agony on Him? And He had not heard" [157]. Why is Pleasant not available to bolster her flagging faith? Where is he at this crucial time? One might surmise that he is spending most of his time with "the adoring women of his flock." Shortly after her arrival in the Alabama town, Helga notices, "Open adoration was the prerogative, the almost religious duty, of the female portion of the flock" [147]. As I have already mentioned, Larsen is careful not to outrightly accuse Pleasant of having committed adultery. In this respect she is faithful to the inclinations of blacks of her generation who were reluctant to cast public indictments against preachers. What Larsen does do is to leave doubts in our minds whether Pleasant is faithful.

Anyway, the community had expected Pleasant to marry Clementine Richards, "a strapping black beauty." She understands the "worth and greatness" of her pastor and thinks Helga must have had a stroke of "good luck" in order to have hooked the great man. But in actuality, it is something profoundly more psychological than good luck that causes Pleasant to marry Helga. Stember was right on point in exposing the "value of a Caucasian appearance" within the context of black society. In her essay entitled "If the Present Looks Like the Past, What Does the Future Look Like?" (1982), Alice Walker notes that "a look at the photographs of the women chosen by our male leaders is, in many ways, chilling" [302]. She points out that though these leaders "affirmed blackness in the abstract," when it came to wife selection these same men chose women based on the "nearness of their complexions to white." This may explain why Pleasant, when we first encounter him, is so far away from his Alabama parish, that "primitive flock" where Clementine with her "Amazon proportions" had been expected to be his betrothed. The women there are not sophisticated enough for him. Clementine is too dark; he needs someone not reminiscent of the African homeland, but someone who will, by virtue of her appearance, enhance his self-esteem and social status.

We will recall Ellison's A. Hebert Bledsoe, who, in the words of the Reverend Barbee, is "a worthy successor to his great friend and it is no accident that his great and intelligent leadership has made him our leading statesman" [131]. The "great friend" referred to in Barbee's speech is none other than Booker T. Washington, the founder of what we can assume is Tuskegee Institute, coincidently also in Alabama. Many historians will argue that Washington was not so much interested in progress for the black race as he was intent on establishing and retaining power. Robert R. Moton succeeded Washington as president of Tuskegee and indeed was there when the young Ellison matriculated in the early 1930s. Conceivably, the character Bledsoe was based on Moton, handpicked by Washington and possessed with the same power-retaining mechanisms of his mentor. There is an unforgettable scene in *Invisible Man* where Bledsoe upbraids the naive narrator and proclaims, "Learn where you are and get yourself power, influence, contacts with powerful and influential people" [142]. A key issue is whether or not that power will be used to engender progress or whether it will be used to maintain the status quo.

Bledsoe is "a leader of his people" and as such is also "the possessor of not one, but *two* Cadillacs, a good salary and a soft, good-looking and creamy-complexioned wife" [99]. While he may "stay in the dark and use" his power for social progress, ostensibly he is preserving things as they are. He is at the helm of an institution designed to keep blacks on a certain social level. He has great power but he uses that power to keep other blacks from attaining it. The narrator admires the fact that this dark-skinned man has a "creamy-complexioned" wife. She is a symbol of the college president's success, an ornament that testifies to her owner's glory. We get no character analysis of her. She is like the Nedeed women of Gloria Naylor's *Linden Hills* (1985), who actually fade into oblivion even as the men they are nurturing achieve increasingly greater social prominence.

In *Linden Hills* we are taken through a series of Nedeed generations, beginning with the first Luther Nedeed, who purchased Luwana Parkerville and then married her. But as might have been expected, she does not gain much in the transition from slave to wife. She has gone from being slave to a slaveowner to being slave to her husband. It is the fourth Nedeed wife, Willa

Prescott, literally imprisoned in her own basement, who discovers letters written on pages in her Bible. Luwana had sought answers from that spiritual text, but her final statement on the matter of her oppressed condition was "There can be no God." The fourth Nedeed wife, who is "imprisoned" by her husband for having borne him a child the wrong complexion, also discovers down in that basement photographs that had been preserved by the third Nedeed wife, Priscilla McGuire. Priscilla had saved the photographs and labeled them "Luther: 1," "Luther: 2," "Luther: 3," and so forth on through the years to chart her son's development until she noticed

> the shadow. As the child grew, the height of his shoulder cast a faint shade across Priscilla McGuire's body. It had started at her lap and then slowly crawled up across her stomach, chest, and neck. What began as a slight, gray film was now deepening into a veil.... It was so easy for the eye to follow the dark lines from the son, across her body to the identical dark lines of the father [208].

In early photographs the child had been seated on Priscilla's lap so that she was "held down" in her position. When the son was six years old, he was standing up in the pictures, allowing for that metaphorical shadow that Naylor uses to symbolize how male oppression, even within a single family, is passed down from father to son much as a sprinter in a relay race hands the baton off to the next runner.

Willa, who thinks she is "losing her mind" anyway, rationalizes that perhaps the "photography wasn't sophisticated" or that these pictures were "only the rejects." As Willa further peruses Priscilla's photographs, she observes the bizarre phenomenon of the veil "now over her chin, drawing closer toward her mouth" [208]. Had Priscilla's son continued to grow and cast a shadow this way? No, we are told, as the photograph series continues:

> *Luther: 20 years.* He had gotten no taller, so why was the veil now across her bottom lip? And in the next, it had finally crept up to cover her mouth.... *Luther: 21 years.* She was no longer recording the growth of a child; the only thing growing in these pictures was her absence [209].

After a point, the son ceased growing, but the shadow continued rising until Priscilla, in a last-ditch effort to maintain her identity, had scrawled the word "me" in the vacant spot where an image of her should have been.

It is significant that Willa finally rises from her basement prison on a Christmas Eve. She physically attacks her husband, and the two of them crash into the Christmas tree, causing it to catch fire and burn the house down. Naylor herself was an evangelist who canvassed the South during the late 1960s. What questions does she now raise concerning issues that she previously must have resolved with a simplistic acceptance of the Bible? The author's concerns are very much like what Lewis expresses when he renders Carol's husband "shocked by Carol's lack of faith" even though he "wasn't quite sure what was the nature of the faith that she lacked" [316]. Carol is an "uneasy and dodging" agnostic, meaning she has not decided how she feels about the prospect of a God and the consequent implications for humanity. She decries the hypocrisy of organized religion but marvels at instances of altruism performed under religious auspices. She refuses to be converted because she has witnessed how men use God for purposes not in the best interests of women, progress, or the common good.

It is astonishing how some fail to see the difficulty. Pleasant does not even know that his wife is reading Anatole France's "The Procurator of Judea" (1892), in which Pontius Pilate can in retirement no longer recall the name Jesus Christ. Laelius Lamia tries to jog his memory: "His name was Jesus; he came from Nazareth, and he was crucified for some crime, I don't quite know what" [26]. Pilot just murmurs, "I cannot call him to mind." France was a humanist and skeptic who wanted to understand the workings of God before conceding a belief in that entity. He was involved in conducting a moral investigation and, in fact, was more deeply committed to moral investigations than many preachers who simply manipulate the Word to their advantage.

In *Roll, Jordan, Roll* (1974), Eugene Genovese portrays black preachers as having "had to make many compromises in order to be able to do the very thing incumbent upon them – to preach the Word" [263]. It is understandable that in order to preach at all, many early black preachers had to present themselves as supportive of the status quo, supportive perhaps of even slavery itself in order for blacks to have access to the Bible and its various interpretations. What Helga eventually finds so disturbing about religion is how it is still used to keep the socially disadvantaged from evolving out of their meager circumstances: She has detected an unfortunate pattern:

> Religion had, after all, its uses. It blunted the perceptions.... Especially it had its uses for the poor – and the blacks.... This, Helga decided, was what ailed the whole Negro race in America, this fatuous belief in the white man's God, this childlike trust in full compensation for all woes and privations in "kingdom come" [159–60].

We can harken back to the white preacher who was invited to the Naxos campus to tell students to "stay in their places." That preacher in effect was an agent in perpetuating slavery, a slavery of the mind this time, yet a slavery just as repressive as the one that was fixed in place by laws and physical chains. Helga had seen him for what he was back then, and she has come to understand how that type can also function through the person of a man like Pleasant.

Helga's husband is no more interested in progressive change than the white preacher in Naxos was. Remember, Helga had been resolved to help uplift Pleasant's community. Even Anderson realized her potential for such endeavors. But the man she chose to marry thinks little of the prospect that she can make a vital social contribution. Carol Kennicott, exuding supreme confidence in the potential of women, goes so far as to proclaim that women have abilities superior to those of men. "We have the plans for a Utopia already made," declares Carol, "we'll produce it; trust us; we're wiser than you" [197]. While it may seem that Lewis overcompensates to make up for the fact that women have had relatively little power, one wonders if indeed women do have better theories about societal development. Helga is bursting with ideas, but as she begins to have children, Pleasant "had rather lost any personal interest in her" [151]. He is mainly interested in reaping the benefits of his exalted position even while his wife drowns in the mire of what she once viewed as a viable alternative.

The author herself at one time thought marriage to an upwardly mobile man would be the answer to all her dreams. Circulating around Harlem as Mrs. Dr. Imes, she reaped the benefits of admission into numerous social circles. But then came Imes's adulterous affairs. "He broke my heart," Larson informs us the author confided to a co-worker. But the issue becomes more than one of marital infidelity. Larsen, like Helga at one time, was determined to make a social impact. She accomplished this feat with the publication of her novels in the late 1920s. When she failed in her attempts to get three additional manuscripts published, she switched careers and, over the course of three decades, contributed valuable humanitarian services as a nurse. Some critics have been quick to assert that this movement away from creative writing is evidence enough to prove she was psychologically disturbed. What has been unfathomable to so many is that Larsen was an individualist who went to great lengths in pursuit of her identity. Her persistence in that endeavor allowed her to share her various gifts with a world that has nevertheless been too slow in comprehending the phenomenon of her brilliant diversity.

John Pearson's Malady: An Incurable Weakness for Women

Nathan Huggins, writing in 1971, criticized Zora Neale Hurston as one whose "great weakness was carelessness or indifference to her art" [131]. Three years later Arthur Davis would characterize *Jonah's Gourd Vine* as a seriously flawed precursor that would nonetheless set the tone for all of her subsequent works. In his analysis of that first novel, Davis asserts:

> We see here the kind of good-will attitude which will characterize all of Miss Hurston's fiction dealing with Negroes. She simply ignored most of the unpleasant racial aspects of Southern life – aspects that have to be recognized if a full picture is to be given. This shutting of the eyes on Miss Hurston's part is a kind of artistic dishonesty that takes away from the work [115–16].

Those critics would have been more appreciative of a novel such as *Gourd Vine* had the author given more attention to the racism that certainly existed in Florida during the 1930s. But what must be remembered is that Hurston was born and raised in the all-black town of Eatonville, where racial discrimination was not an everyday factor of life. Blacks held prominent positions such as mayor and postmaster. To a large extent, Hurston was in the enviable position to be able to view life beyond the boundaries of race. What she discovered were universal aspects of human nature that indeed cut across race lines and provide us with what Robert Hemenway has referred to as "a persistent tension . . . between the institutions of society, such as marriage or the church, and the individual's need for self-expression" ["Flying Lark" 142]. Rather than be appalled at Hurston's lack of attention to racism, the earlier critics could have found cause to celebrate a black woman concerned with the issue of female self-discovery in the midst of a world where institutionalized sexism predominates.

It is, moreover, a well-conceded fact now that Hurston's work is emblematic of an extraordinarily talented artist. Of special importance is the manner in which she infused folklore in her telling of the story. James Weldon Johnson, in his preface to *God's Trombones* (1927), spoke highly of the "old-time Negro preacher" as someone who had not yet been given his due. The black preacher, according to Johnson, was a "man of positive genius" who "knew the secret of oratory." He was the consummate poet. It is somewhat curious, however, that Johnson chose to render his sermons using standard English, explaining that black dialect had limitations "not due to any defect of the dialect as dialect, but to the mould of convention in which Negro dialect in the United States has been set, to the fixing effects of its long association with the Negro only as a happy-go-lucky or a forlorn figure" [7]. It was not so much that Johnson thought black dialect an inferior way of speaking. After all, he had been a "pupil" of Paul Laurence Dunbar. Johnson acknowledged, "The passing of dialect as a medium for Negro poetry will be an actual loss, for in it many beautiful things can be done, and done best" [8]. Johnson eliminated dialect from his sermons in verse because he did not want the society-based limitation of strictly pathos or humor to be the only way of perceiving the essence of what the sermons had to convey. It was his view that "*traditional* Negro dialect as a form for Aframerican poets is absolutely dead" [8]. Considering that he also wrote his only novel, *The Autobiography of an Ex-Coloured Man* (1912), using standard English, we can conclude that the limitation he saw to using dialect in poetry was also perceived by him as a limitation when it came to writing prose fiction. Needless to say, Hurston did not share Johnson's opinion about dialect being "absolutely dead."

In "The Creation," Johnson traces, in sermon form, the creation of earth and its surrounding elements to the point where God has decided to make a man:

> Up from the bed of the river
> God scooped the clay;
> And by the bank of the river
> He kneeled him down;
> And there the great God Almighty
> Who lit the sun and fixed it in the sky,
> Who flung the stars to the most far corner of the night,
> Who rounded the earth in the middle of his hand;
> This great God,
> Like a mammy bending over her baby,
> Kneeled down in the dust
> Toiling over a lump of clay
> Till he shaped it in his own image [20].

Now I should mention that I grew up in the late 1950s and early 1960s, listening to my mother and aunts reciting that poem in its entirety. They were all public school teachers, and they recited it from memory with intense pride in the language style Johnson had selected. The narrator of *Ex-Coloured Man* tells of a preacher named John Brown who "knew all the arts and tricks of oratory, the modulation of the voice to almost a whisper, the pause for effect, the rise through light, rapid-fire sentences to the terrific, thundering outburst of an electrifying climax. . . . Eloquence consists more in the manner of saying than in what is said. It is largely a matter of tone pictures" [175–76]. All of the figures of speech (metaphor, personification, and simile) are evident in that excerpt from "The Creation." It is through words, in fact, that we obtain a vivid picture of God – like the omnipresent mammy of slavery times – in love with the object of His nurturing. Dialect would not have served the purpose of my relatives in their efforts to present black culture as being on a par with other cultures in America. Like Johnson, they were interested in conveying articulateness as they sought to foster black pride. What I would come to realize later, through literary reminders from Hurston, is that the language free of dialect is but a distilled version of the Southern black preacher's delivery.

I should not have needed those reminders because I had spent a significant portion of my youth growing up in rural Virginia and had often heard the verbal geniuses in the pulpit on Sunday mornings. Yet I would wager that most of the parishioners there in Charles City, Virginia, could listen and admire the extraordinary gifts of their preachers without really knowing how to convert those sermons to the written word. At this task Hurston was especially adept as through the voice of the Reverend John Pearson she renders her version of God at the point where He is about to create man:

> Now I'm ready to make man
> Aa-aah!
> Who shall I make him after? Ha!
> Worlds within worlds begin to wheel and roll
> De Sun, Ah!
> Gethered up de fiery skirts of her garments
> And wheeled around de throne, Ah!
> Saying, Ah, make man after me, ha!
> God gazed upon the sun
> And sent her back to her blood-red socket
> And shook His head, ha!
> De Moon, ha!
> Grabbed up de reins of de tides.
> And dragged a thousand seas behind her
> As she walked around de throne
> Ah-h, please make man after me
> But God said "NO!"
> De stars bust out from their diamond sockets
> And circled de glitterin' throne cryin'
> A-aah! Make man after me
> God said, "NO!"
> I'll make man in my own image, ha! [176]

That excerpt is taken in part from a sermon delivered by the Reverend C.C. Lovelace in Eau Gallie, Florida, on May 3, 1929. It appears in varied form in several of Hurston's works, including *Mules and Men* (1935) and the posthumously published folklore collection, *The Sanctified Church* (1981). The creation sermon as presented by Hurston is noticeably different from Johnson's version. It is not as distilled and the elements of black culture are more vivid. The sun and stars of Johnson's version become, when we get to Hurston, a Sun and Moon with magnificent powers of their own, in competition with God for the chance to have man patterned after them. First the Sun and then the Moon present their accoutrements in the game of one-upmanship. The incomplete suffixes and the use of "de" instead of "the" reflect the language of the masses, a technique that the astute Southern rural preacher knew how to employ regardless of how advanced his own formal education might have been. Hurston, in her glossary section of *Mules*, explains the preacher's use of the interjections "Ah!" and "ha!" as "a breathing device, done rhythmically to punctuate the lines" [255]. Yet, however in tune with the masses he was, there was still a strong tendency for the congregation to view him as the right hand of God. And church members were vigilant in their search for evidence to support this perspective. Part of Pearson's response is to go beyond the mere recitation of words from the Bible. He actually shows his congregation – down to the grunt and groan – how God agonized over the decision to make a man.

How did Pearson come by his oratory skill? Hurston wants us to understand that he acquired it from two distinct sources. One source is the natural setting of his early youth in Notasulga, where he one day comes upon a train depot and at first thinks it is a cotton gin. A train approaches, and it is obvious to those around him that he is terrified at the "fiery-lunged monster." "Hey, dere, big-un," a man loitering at the station asks John, "you ain't never seed nothin' dangerous lookin' lak dat befo', is yuh?" [16]. John admits, "Hit sho look frightenin'," but he also observes, "Hits uh pretty thing." Not at all knowledgeable about the huge machine, he nevertheless is endowed with a firm appreciation of it. Unlike the loiterer, who pretends to know all there is to know about trains (while actually knowing very little at all), John acknowledges his ignorance but senses, in ways that others cannot, a vital significance to this thing that is so much a mystery to him. As the train roars off, John tells his fellow bystander, "Ah lakted dat. It say something but Ah ain't heered it 'nough tuh tell whut it say yit" [16]. The acquaintance tells John, "It don't say nothin'," to which John vehemently replies, "Naw, it say some words too. Ahm comin' heah plenty mo' times and den Ah tell yuh whut it say" [16].

John is possessed with the requisite intuition. We had gotten a hint of this earlier when "the Big Creek thundered among its rocks and whirled on down. So John sat on the foot-log and made some words to go with the drums of the Creek" [12]. He is one with his natural surroundings and in the case of the creek, he has had access to it so much and is so familiar with its rhythms that he no longer has difficulty supplying words for its drums. The creek is a part of his cultural habitat as the train itself will become after he has had enough experience with its sounds. John will learn that the train comes into the station twice a day, and before long his total being is in unison with the engine's roar, the drivers chanting "Opelika-black-and-dirty," and the whistle blaring, "Wah-hoom! Wahup, wahup!"

As much as Richard Wright appears to have disliked Hurston's style of writing black dialect, he does, in *Black Boy* (1945), convey a message about trains that is similar to Hurston's use of this key folkloric tool. The train symbolizes escape from a repressive South to the North, where there was deemed at one time to be more opportunity for individualistic expression. As Wright concludes that first installment of his autobiography, he speaks of the "hostile and forbidding" South from which he is about to escape because, as he puts it, "I had somehow gotten the idea that life could be different, could be lived in a fuller and richer manner" [281]. John Pearson has an inkling of the train's vast significance when he asks the pertinent question, "Whar it gwine?" His fellow bystander answers, "Eve'y which and whar," which on the surface seems to be a statement of supreme ignorance. The bystander does not know where the train is going and his answer is, once again, the evidence of his ineptness with regard to such matters. But as we consider the reasons why blacks, in such large numbers, left their Southern localities, the bystander deserves some credence. Many blacks fled in a semiorganized fashion to particular Northern metropolises such as Chicago, Detroit, and New York. Others fled just to get out. Escape to anywhere was the priority to avoid a debt trap, to escape a brutal lynching, or just to hold on to one's sanity.

Hurston, of course, believed that moral backwardness was not a feature of just one race. So when John, at seventeen years of age, has to leave the Beasley farm, it is not so much because he cannot stand whites as it is that he can no longer tolerate his own stepfather, Ned Crittenden. When John's mother, Amy, had fed her children before feeding Ned, that incensed husband whipped her across her head and back, kneed her in the stomach, and was at the point of choking her to death when John floored him with a single punch. The son was only defending his mother, but Ned has had his pride destroyed by no less than a boy, albeit a powerfully built boy who, physically speaking, is well into his young manhood. After the family has moved to the Shelby plantation, the two still harbor animosity towards each other, so that when Ned orders John to take the plow and John fails to move fast enough, the stepfather relishes the opportunity to be vindictive, threatening, "Don't set dere and answer me. When Ah speak, you move!" [45]. John answers anyway, saying he does not "run fuh nobody." This is the encounter where John realizes he has just about reached his limit with Ned's troubling behavior.

Ned will try again to establish his authority over John, demanding on one occasion, "Drop dem britches below yo' hocks, and git down on yo' knees" [46]. He is determined to whip John, but this stepson is equal to the challenge and delivers a threat of his own: "Ah done promised Gawd and uh couple uh other men tuh stomp yo' guts out nex' time you raise yo' hand tuh me" [46]. Ned leaves, vowing to return with his shotgun. Although the stepfather does not follow through with his threat, John knows he himself must leave, escape this life-style, and venture to the other side of the creek, where he promises himself, "Ahm gointer be somebody."

One source for John's talent was the rural environment within which he was nurtured. But the talent he had then was still a raw talent. It is Lucy Potts, from the "right side" of the creek, who further nurtures and develops him into the preacher who will have the power of words to mesmerize members of Zion Hope Baptist Church. He begins courting her while she is a mere fourteen years old. *Gourd Vine* is largely autobiographical. In Hurston's actual autobiography, *Dust Tracks on a Road* (1942), she tells how her father, a "tall, heavy-muscled mulatto," met her mother, the Lucy Potts after whom John's wife in the novel is named.

> He had been born near Notasulga, Alabama, in an outlying district of landless Negroes, and whites not too much better off. It was "over the creek," which was just like saying on the wrong side of the railroad tracks. John Hurston had learned to read and write somehow between

cotton-choppings and cotton-picking, and it might have satisfied him in a way. But somehow he took to going to Macedonia Baptist Church on the right side of the creek. He went one time, and met up with dark-brown Lucy Ann Potts, of the land-owning Richard Potts, which might have given him the going habit [20].

Hurston goes on to mention that, at the time, her father was twenty while her mother, in line with the novel's depiction, was only fourteen. In other words, he was a man courting a girl, a phenomenon not beyond the bounds of late nineteenth-century American tradition.

We could defend that way of life as having been appropriate for those times. John Hurston's world was not technologically advanced. White men needed only the basics as far as education was concerned. Black men were afforded even less. The woman's role, or "girl's" in the case of Lucy Potts, was to maintain the home, raise the children, do the cooking. And certainly, extensive formal education was not deemed a prerequisite in order for women to perform those responsibilities. Yet, in *Dust Tracks*, Hurston describes her mother as the "smartest black girl" in the area, a theme the author had already presented in *Gourd Vine* when she has John confide to Lucy, "Wisht Ah could speak pieces lak you do" [32]. A certain amount of social indoctrination mixed in with sincere love and devotion prompts Lucy to respond, "You kin speak 'em better'n me . . . you got uh good voice for speakin'" [32]. She wants to encourage the man who will one day be the head of her household, the father of her children, the "prop" for her "eve'y leanin' side." This indeed is how John describes himself.

Joe Starks, of *Their Eyes*, is also in part based on Hurston's father. When Joe first arrives in Eatonville, he exudes leadership potential, the way he carries himself and strives to be a "big voice." Before long he is giving speeches, but some townspeople want to hear what his wife has to say. Joe abruptly puts her in her place, declaring, "Ah never married her for nothin' lak dat. She's uh woman and her place is in de home" [69]. He has saved her from the hard labor that Logan was planning, and his desire is to make her "lak a lady." Just as John has envisioned with Lucy, Joe wants to assume his place at the head of the household. With his power confirmed, he then will prop Janie up, all the while making her into little more than an ornament.

In an essay entitled "Saving the Life That Is Your Own" (1976), Alice Walker investigates the socially imposed functions of women. Throughout history, they have been regarded either in terms of the labor they can supply or the position they can fill as "ladies." Commenting on how she had been introduced to *Their Eyes* at a relatively late stage in her life, she goes on to say that the novel now is as necessary to her as "air and water." In fact she also includes a poem ("Janie Crawford") that praises the main protagonist for finally rejecting the emotionally debilitating gender roles.

Janie's grandmother had warned her "de nigger woman is de mule uh de world" [29]. That grandmother had lived during the time of slavery, when blacks were an unpaid, exploitable labor pool. In her estimation, although black men were given the most physically difficult tasks, they shifted that burden to black women. Within the system of slavery, there existed a subsystem of a different kind of slavery where those men in bondage themselves often subjected their women to another type of bondage, that of male dominance over the female. To a large extent it was a simple matter of the man being stronger and thereby able to force his designs on the physically "weaker" sex. It was a meager attempt to imitate the perceived relationships between white males and their respective white female mates.

What was impossible for the black man to achieve under the institution of slavery was the assurance that black women could be treated as ladies. Such a characterization would have been totally against the grain of what the system sought to perpetuate with its assignment of slaves as chattel property. To be a lady or, in Barbara Welter's words, a participant in the "cult of true womanhood" during slavery, one had to be a white woman. Once slavery had ended, however, Janie's grandmother Nanny presumed that being a lady was feasible now, even for a black woman, just as long as she did not wind up marrying a man who would revert back to the slavery period treatment of women as mules. Nanny cannot be blamed for her myopia, for practically any situation would have been better for her granddaughter than what that grandmother experienced as a slave. From Nanny's perspective, being a lady represents the pinnacle of female success.

The bubble begins to burst as we analyze the tenets Welter ascribes to the condition of so-called true womanhood. Specifying the period from 1820 to the Civil War, Welter informs us that "the attributes of True Womanhood, by which a woman judged herself and was judged by her husband, her neighbors and society, could be divided into four cardinal virtues—piety, purity, submissiveness and domesticity" [21], a demanding set of requirements that, even if carried out successfully, would relegate woman to the position of a glorified inmate in a socially acceptable prison. Hazel Carby has suggested that even during the time of slavery, white women "were not living embodiments of true womanhood" [23]. The cult of true womanhood was just that, a cult, a functional facade that enabled white men to maintain power over slaves and also white women, who in particular knew the risks they would take if they deviated too much from societal expectations.

Adrienne Rich has conducted her own examination of the control exerted by white male authority figures, including legislators, jurists, and preachers. In her essay "Disloyal to Civilization" (1978), she calls for drastic change "not to an extension of tokenism to include more women in existing social structures, but to a profound transformation of world society and of human relationships" [279]. Every woman, she argues, should at the very least be "self-identifying and self-defining." The "lady or mule" stipulation for women would no longer have a place in Rich's proposed new world order, where the masses of women would define their own roles.

In the "old" world order, when John confides to Lucy his wish that he could be as good a public speaker as her, she automatically responds that he can do better than her. She has been indoctrinated to believe this is the case. And even if she believed that her potential for public speaking far exceeded his, what were the opportunities for a black woman speaker? Certainly not politics. Women had not yet been afforded their right to vote. Teaching positions at most traditionally black colleges were limited to instructorships in home economics, not a very encouraging prospect for someone of Lucy's intellectual capacity. And then there is the matter of theology itself. Writing from her own experiences about what the comparative educational allowances were in this field during a time that coincides with the period when John and Lucy were first getting together, Anna Julia Cooper exposed the following double standard:

> A boy, however meager his equipment and shallow his pretentions, had only to declare a floating intention to study theology and he could get all the support, encouragement and stimulus he needed, be absolved from work and invested beforehand with all the dignity of his far away office. While a self-supporting girl had to struggle . . . working after school hours to keep up with her board bills, and actually to fight her way against positive discouragements to the higher education; till one such girl one day flared out and told the principal "the only mission opening before a girl in his school was to marry one of those candidates" [77].

So the opportunities were indeed very limited for women. When Lucy tells John he can speak better than her, she is responding as a female member of that world society Rich finds so much in need of radical transformation.

It is worthwhile to analyze John's response to being a male in the old world society. He readily admits that his vocabulary is much more limited than Lucy's, and he wants to know how she has managed to learn so much. Lucy has been fortunate to have had a family that encouraged her to a certain extent. The Pottses were a prominent family in town and as such they fostered educational attainment, even for their daughter. But according to Hurston, her mother, Lucy Potts, was extremely smart. The novel's Lucy also possesses a keen intellect and determination. In answer to John's question concerning when she could ever have managed to learn so much, Lucy shares with him that she accomplishes it "in de night time round home after Ah git thru wid mah lessons" [32]. She is perhaps possessed with the workaholic tendencies that have characterized some of our most successful American leaders. Or it may be that workaholism is not an appropriate assessment. She may have had a love for such learning to the extent that it was not a labor at all. It may have easily been within her natural abilities to be one of the greatest orators of all time.

As if to argue for the position that women can do anything men can do, Hurston has John challenge Lucy to a footrace. They race a considerable distance to a sweet gum tree. John wins, but only by a "foot or two that he had gained with difficulty" [33]. In one of the most symbolic statements in the novel, Lucy counters her defeat, saying, "Yeah, you beat me, but look how much mo' legs you got to run wid.... Bet if Ah had dem legs nobody couldn't never outrun me" [33]. Recall that John is tall, strong, in his male prime, and had leveled his stepfather with a single punch. What are the implications of the fact that, in a footrace, he can only beat Lucy by a foot or two, Lucy who at this point in the novel is only twelve years old? Hurston is commenting on the nature of woman's potential. Woman is the physical and intellectual equal of man. And efforts to deny this reality do a disservice to any attempts at understanding and bettering those "human relationships" between the sexes to which Rich refers. John, who has actually started courting Lucy in spite of her young age, renders what could well be the second most symbolic statement in the novel when he says, "You ain't got many mo' days tuh be studyin' of nights. Den whut you gwine do wid yo'self?" [32]. The assumption is that Lucy's formal education will soon come to an end and she will become involved in the activity of searching for a man to "take care of her" while she gives birth to and raises all the children he wants. This is John's response to being a male in world society, only it takes the shape of a social edict that had been cast in stone from the very beginnings of human existence, an edict with regard to which women had had very little say-so.

In all fairness to John, he does early on seem rather oblivious to the role that he nonetheless personifies. He gets a late start in terms of any extensive interaction with the opposite sex. As a sixteen-year-old still living on the "wrong side" of the Big Creek, he dreams of the other side, where "maybe people had lots of daughters." He ponders, "No telling how many girls might be living on the new and shiny side" [12]. His dreams recall how sex therapists Masters and Johnson describe the onset of puberty. Those therapists explain, "Rising hormone levels contribute to an activation of sexual sensations and erotic thoughts and dreams for boys and girls" [193]. Once on the other side of the creek at the Pearson plantation, John becomes involved in the late evening games—"Hide the Switch" and "Hide and Seek"—that the young people play, games that are actually rites of sexual initiation. Only the games are somewhat lopsided in that all of the girls want to be "whipped" by John in the former game, and then in the latter game, the girls all want to hide with him. A case in point is Phrony, a "womanish fourteen-year-old" who, when it is time to hide, pulls John aside and advises him in a manner that would have been difficult for many an adolescent male to resist:

> "Ah'll show yuh uh good place tuh hide," she whispered, "nobody can't find yuh."
> She dragged him off the path to the right and round and about to a clump of sumac overrun with wild grape vines.
> "Right under heah," she panted from running, "nobody can't find yuh."
> "Whar you goin' hide yuhself?" John asked as he crept into the arboreal cave.
> "Iss plenty room," Phrony whispered. "Us bofe kin hide in heah."
> She crept in also and leaned heavily upon John, giggling and giggling as the counting went on [22].

When the counting is finished and all the adolescents race to get to base before they are tagged, the counting starts again, and this time Mehaley intercepts John from Phrony and has her turn at showing him a good place to hide. John "wanted to pit his strength and speed against the boy who was counting. He wanted to practise running, but he felt a flavor come out from Mehaley" [23]. Before he is able to regain control of his faculties, he is off hiding with her in the hay, where she, like Phrony before her, leans against him. She rubs his hair and one wonders what else. When they return to the site of the game, Minnie is awaiting her turn.

Hurston wants us to know that though John is a commoner, he is an extraordinarily attractive man whose biological father, Alf Pearson, is white. Lucy, on the other hand, is a social elite. It is John's handsomeness that has made Lucy accessible to him. Before he and Lucy finally wed, distractive females continue to make themselves available. There is Exie and Big 'Oman, and then after John and Lucy marry, there are more rendezvous with Big 'Oman and Mehaley and Delphine, who drift into town from Opelika. Referring to John by his boyhood name, Darwin Turner concludes, "John Buddy does not create situations intentionally. Instead, he reacts to fortune's winds, which most often emanate from the gusty pantings of lustful women" [100]. Remember that the character John is largely based on Hurston's father. Although

John Hurston certainly had his faults, including the disposition to be a philanderer, one senses an urge on the part of the daughter to romanticize what we might otherwise consider a totally tragic condition.

Tea Cake Woods, in *Their Eyes*, stands out as another man who appeals to any number of women. We recall a wrestling bout he has with the precocious Nunkie. We also remember how he is inclined to disappear for extended periods to take in various forms of social entertainment. Tea Cake is a charmer. But the literary world would have to wait until *Seraph on the Suwanee* (1948) in order to see the likes of one with the physical attributes of John Pearson.

> Jim Meserve was very handsome too, and had stirred the hearts of practically every single girl in town. Caps were set to catch the laughing stranger. . . . He had the thick head of curly hair, deep blue eyes with long black lashes . . . dimples in his lean cheeks, white strong teeth set in a chaffing mouth [8].

Hurston was undoubtedly concerned about the impact that physical beauty in a man had on the nature of his relationships.

John is so overwhelming, in fact, that a stranger meets him just once and immediately wants to introduce him to his sister. That stranger tries his best to encourage John, urging him, "She's uh fine lookin', portly 'oman; you better come 'long" [103]. This is the effect John has on some men. When he first arrives at the Pearson plantation, he has to be prodded to attend social functions. It is Exie who tells him, "De boys neither de gals don't do 'round when you ain't dere lak dey do when yo' is" [55]. Much of this appeal has to do with his striking personality. He enjoys life, is widely liked, and is thought essential for any social gathering.

Nevertheless, John and Lucy wed, and once they begin having children, the couple relocates to Eatonville, that town where, reminiscent of Joe Starks, John has come to believe "uh man kin be sumpin' heah 'thout folks tramplin' all over yuh" [107]. He wants to make his mark. Note, however, that Eatonville, as an up-and-coming town, was a place where a *man* could "be sumpin'." The black woman, even within the context of this all-black society, must wait until another time for her chance at equal opportunity.

When John declares that he has been called to preach, the church "boiled over with approval." But does the congregation approve because of his oratorical skills? Few at this point have even heard him preach. Does the congregation accept him because they perceive an innate goodness in him? He has not done anything to show himself to be more moral than other men. What has happened is that John has come into an awareness of his power over others. He has what contemporary "how to succeed" counselors would call presence. Joe Starks of *Their Eyes*, pops into the fledgling town, takes the initiative in a few things, and then, almost at once, the town believes that there can be no one better for the job of mayor. He has "wowed" them. Hurston's own father was mayor of Eatonville for three terms, and Hemenway, her biographer, informs us: "John Hurston was one of the strongest men in the village, two hundred pounds of hard muscle, known for his bravery, leadership, and powerful, poetical preaching. A family legend told how he once 'cold-conked' a mule with his fist" [14].

Hurston's father, it seems, became larger than life as he took on the proportions of a folkloric hero. We see this carried out to an even greater extreme in Hurston's third novel, *Moses, Man of the Mountain* (1939), where the traditional Moses is given many of the attributes of a black Southern preacher. Ruthe Sheffey assesses:

> In this book Moses is more than chief preacher and teacher; he is the original conjurer and two-headed doctor whose staff changes to a snake and who has the power to change water to blood, to bring a plague of frogs on Egypt, leprosy on Miriam, and death on Aaron. Hurston recognized these hoodoo powers as the hidden, perhaps lost, substratum of the Southern black church, so that Moses combines his function as chief hoodoo hougan with that as Afro-American preacher/ leader [213].

Hurston was acutely aware of how Western civilization has seemed to ignore the full implication of Genesis 10:1, where Noah's sons are enumerated. There is Japheth, whose offspring evolved into the Indo-Europeans, who developed a reputation in the field of philosophy. Shem was the progenitor of a large Jewish nation famous for its contributions to religious evolutions. All Ham (the other son of Noah) is famous for is a curse that has been used throughout the millennia as an excuse to oppress blacks in one way or another. The task, as Hurston saw it, was one of resurrecting an ignored culture even as she was critical of the black men she saw as harbingers of control.

It is obvious that a large part of Hurston wants to come to John's defense. She has already portrayed him as a man overly burdened with temptation. By the time he and Lucy have had seven children together (Hurston's mother and father had eight), he still has the proclivity to roam, but the author is quick to supply him with excuses. When his youngest daughter, Isis, contracts typhoid fever, he flees to Tampa because he is "gutted with grief." Hattie Tyson, who already had designs on him, joins him there and sees to it that he "forgot about the dying Isis." In a manner of speaking, she has helped him through his grief and when he returns to Eatonville, he is overjoyed to discover that Isis has survived her illness after all.

John comes across as one of the author's most pathetic characters. As though he can make up for the fact that he disappeared during that crucial time, he gives Lucy a new dress and a pineapple, his version of a peace offering. And though Lucy accepts the two items, we know how ludicrous it would be to assume that a pineapple is adequate compensation for desertion and infidelity. The tendering of the dress serves also to remind us of John's inadequacy. The dress symbolizes a Lucy who knows and accepts her place in their marriage. Earlier, when she had tried to bring up the issue of his adulterous affairs, he had summarily responded, "Don't tell me 'bout dem trashy women Ah lusts after once in uh while. Dey's less dan leaves uh grass" [111]. We see how he has divided women into two classes. He wants his wife on a pedestal, but he spends an enormous amount of time giving the "other type" of woman his attention.

Ponder, as well, the nature of this "respect" that John would accord Lucy. It consists of one failed attempt after another to harness his philandering ways, his willingness to continually offer excuses, and his ongoing insistence that she give him the proverbial "one more chance." Long before he had rendered his explanation about "trashy women," Lucy asked him, "What make yuh fool wid scrubs lak Big 'Oman and de rest of 'em?" [88]. On that occasion, John's reply was:

Dat's de brute-beast in me, but Ah sho aim tuh live clean from dis on
if you 'low me one mo' chance. Don't tongue-lash me – jes' try me and
see. Here you done had three younguns fuh me and fixin' have uh
'nother. Try me Lucy [88].

He makes an interesting point as he compares himself to a wild
animal. Humankind is part of the animal kingdom. Many, however, believe that people are morally superior to other species of
the animal world. With John's appeal that the beast lives in him –
closer to a Darwinian than a biblical analysis – the distinction between humans and others of the animal kingdom becomes blurred,
bringing into question those issues concerning the intellect, the
soul, and the capacity of human beings to act in ways that are
more morally right than wrong.

In his controversial *And the Walls Came Tumbling Down*
(1989), Ralph Abernathy conveyed the earthshattering news that
his best friend, Martin Luther King, Jr., had had adulterous relationships. Stressing that "all of us" at the Southern Christian
Leadership Conference had "our weak moments," Abernathy
went on to say, "I don't think it had anything to do with our
respective views of what was right or wrong" [471]. Worse sins,
he said, were "hatred and a cold disregard for others." In all the
criticism that Abernathy received for writing about this aspect of
King's character, it is overlooked that he offered a compelling
defense. An ordained minister himself, Abernathy portrayed
King as

> a man who attracted women, even when he didn't intend to, and at-
> tracted them in droves. Part of his appeal was his predominant role in
> the black community and part of it was personal. During the last ten
> years of his life, Martin Luther King was the most important black
> man in America. Indeed, he was the most important leader our people
> had seen in many generations, probably the most important ever. That
> fact alone endowed him with an aura of power and greatness that
> women found very appealing. He was a hero – the greatest hero of his
> age – and women are always attracted to a hero [471].

It is useful to compare that depiction of King to Hurston's father
and the rendition of him we receive in *Gourd Vine*. These are all
men of power and extreme attractiveness far beyond that of
average men. We might add the biblical David to that list not only
because he had to withstand a varied assortment of pressures

associated with being the king of Israel but also because of the adultery that he committed with Bathsheba, the wife of one of his own soldiers. The same David whom God so favored that He gave him power to kill the giant Goliath was weak enough to conduct an illicit affair with another man's wife and then compound the moral problem by seeing to it that her husband was sent into battle to be killed.

Abernathy made an important point when he talked about the pressures of great men and their need for a means of escape from the routine of their daily lives. But I am afraid that he puts too much blame on the women who fall prey to men with extraordinary power. Abernathy maintained that, for the sake of the Civil Rights Movement, he tried to persuade King to stop having affairs. In one instance, King was quoted as having said, "The FBI can do whatever they please, but I have no intention of cutting off this relationship" [475]. Of course, the FBI under J. Edgar Hoover sought to discredit King in whatever way it could; such activities have no place in a free society. But in this era of family values and assessments of high-profile citizens' characters, it is proper to make relevant evaluations of how they conduct their private lives, especially if those lives amount to a profound hypocrisy. King had his own theory about infidelity; it is curious that Abernathy would mention King had such a theory, but then decline to tell us what that theory was. One can only conclude that in revealing the theory he might have shed detrimental light on how King himself perceived the place of women as compared to men in society.

In her treatise exploring the causes and consequences of marital infidelity, Emily Brown has maintained that "the roots of sexual addiction extend back to childhood experiences of abuse or extreme neglect which have never been reconciled. Dysfunctional sexual and relationship patterns were pervasive in the family of origin, and the addict learned to substitute brief sexual highs for feelings of emptiness, isolation, shame, and low self-esteem" [117]. As we contemplate John's background and consider that his biological father was a white man who did not help raise him, then it is understandable how the boy might have felt neglected. In his frequent bouts of fury, Ned Crittenden was not above reminding Amy in John's presence, "Ahm de pappy uh all but dat one" [3].

The stepfather wound up resenting the fact that this oldest boy was different from his own children. John's skin was lighter and, as far as Ned was concerned, that was reason enough to make him an outcast. Although John ventures to the other side of the creek, his sense of alienation is not allowed to subside. True, girls on the Pearson plantation are awestricken in his presence. In addition, the more refined Lucy is also attracted to him. But Lucy's mother is another case. She confronts John and tells him, "Ah ain't raisin' no gals tuh throw 'way on trash" [68]. It is more than coincidence that John, in turn, will come to view certain women as Lucy's mother does. In a large sense he wants to be like those who are in such a position that they can look down on others. Hurston thus creates a character with the basic human flaw that Faulkner, two years later, would investigate in *Absalom, Absalom!* In that tale we have another plantation, and Thomas Sutpen's father is a laborer there. Faulkner makes it clear that this boy is "still innocent" when the father sends him to deliver a message to "the big house." Young Thomas has no idea what sort of work his father does on the plantation. Furthermore, he is not even sure that he could comprehend the message that he is to deliver. What he does understand is that because he is poor "he had been told to go around to the back door even before he could state his errand" [233]. And from a boy's perspective, we are told how the rejection felt. "It was like he might have been sent with a lump of lead or even a few molded bullets so that the man who owned the fine rifle could shoot it, and the man came to the door and told him to leave the bullets on a stump at the edge of the woods, not even letting him come close enough to look at the rifle" [234]. To get the full impact of that analogy, it must be noted that Faulkner loved hunting so much that it almost kept him from going to pick up his Nobel Prize in 1949. Had Faulkner been forced to deliver bullets in this way, his sense of alienation would have been extreme; correspondingly, Sutpen's reaction is that of one who has been devastated.

The greatest tragedy conveyed in that novel, however, is how the man Sutpen can inflict on others what he had experienced when he was a boy. Like Hurston's heroic frontiersmen, he is rugged and apparently inclined toward some vague belief in human equality because he engages in the ritual of friendly wrestling matches with slaves he has acquired on what is now his plantation. But Sutpen fights valiantly in the Civil War to preserve the peculiar institution. He sires an illegitimate child by one of his slaves, which is no better, in moral terms, than his desertion of a Haitian wife because he learns that she has black blood. When he marries Ellen Coldfield, it is not for love but to facilitate the design he conceived when he, as a boy, had been turned away from the front door. He marries her because she is from an upstanding family and will consequently serve as a crucial stepping-stone.

When John courts Lucy and first sees her parents' home, he

> noted the prosperous look of the Potts place. It was different from every other Negro's place that he had ever seen. Flowers in the yard among whitewashed rocks. Tobacco hanging up to dry. Peanuts drying on white cloth in the sun. A smoke-house, a spring-house, a swing under a china-berry tree, bucket flowers on the porch [68].

John is thoroughly impressed and hopes to have the same type of material success. Just as Sutpen sees Ellen Coldfield as his avenue to material prosperity and social acceptance, John sees Lucy as his vehicle up the socioeconomic ladder. The irony is that in spite of these women being essential to their husbands' progress, they are left far behind in terms of having attained any semblance of social equality for themselves.

As important as Ellen is to Sutpen's prospects for rising in society, we are told that he sought her out only after he had "exhausted the possibilities of the families of the men with whom he had hunted and gambled" [42]. By the time he came out of the wilderness and made it to Jefferson, Mississippi, he had "come to town to find a wife exactly as he would have gone to the Memphis market to buy livestock or slaves" [42]. And the limited voice that Ellen has in his undertakings is evidence that though as a Southern white woman she is provided with a pedestal, she is as powerless as those slaves to whom Faulkner compared her.

The "vital Lucy," as Hurston calls her, is so crucial a factor in John's rise that it is hard to imagine him surviving at all without someone of her caliber supporting his every effort. "Ah'll never be 'ginst yuh, John" [119], she assures him even in the midst of his philandering episodes. He has gotten such a reputation because of his weakness for women that church officials are about to dismiss him. It is Lucy who does the calculating and then perceptively advises:

> You preach uh sermon on yo'self, and you call tuh they remembrance some uh de good things you done, so they kin put it long side de other and when you lookin' at two things at de same time neither one of 'em don't look so big, but don't tell uh lie, John. If youse guilty you don't need tuh git up dere and put yo' own name on de sign post uh scorn, but don't say you didn't do it neither. Whut you say, let it be de truth. Dat what comes from de heart will sho reach de heart agin [122].

What Lucy understands is the impulse in most people to accept humanness in leaders. In 1988, it was the approach that televangelist Jimmy Swaggart took once the public became aware of his indiscretions with women. As soon as he appeared on the television screen, crying, pleading, "I have sinned against you, Lord," we saw him in all his human frailty; many sympathized so much that they thought it would be appropriate if he continued his ministry. He was forgiven as he laid himself bare to "take the fall" even as his family looked on, humiliated but there, nonetheless, to help him carry on.

We were appalled upon learning that Swaggart had been caught yet again, soliciting sex from a prostitute. How could he betray the wife who had stood behind him so loyally? We are likewise appalled when John hits Lucy on her deathbed. All she had wanted was for him to "keep ole Hattie Tyson's letters out dis house where mah chillun kin git holt of 'em" [128]. His first response is a crude, "Shet up!" followed by the rationalizing and excuse-making that have characterized his feelings on this subject throughout their marriage. "'Tain't nothin' Ah hate lak gittin' sin throwed in mah face dat done got cold," he further declares, "You jus' uh hold-back tuh me nohow" [128]. Both parts of his statement are utterly fallacious. The issue of his adultery is not the frivolous dredging up of the past by a spiteful spouse. It has been an ugly mark on their union from beginning to end. And how he can twist his mouth to call her a hold-back is beyond any mechanism of legitimate logic.

Troy Maxson, in August Wilson's play *Fences* (1986), sheds some light on the absurdity of John's assertions. Married to a woman who has, for eighteen years, kept him away from prison and overindulgence in alcohol, Troy nevertheless has an adulterous affair. He explains it using baseball terminology:

> You born with two strikes on you before you come to the plate. You got to guard it closely . . . always looking for the curve-ball on the inside corner. You can't afford to let none get past you. You can't afford a call strike. If you going down . . . you going down swinging [69].

He sounds like someone going through a midlife crisis, needing to confirm his virility. Yet his problem is more than that. Emily Brown wants us to look to the nature of one's childhood development (especially where there was neglect and lowered self-esteem) as a means of assessing later adultery. By Troy's account, his father was such a brutal man that by the age of fourteen, the boy was compelled to leave home. His mother had already deserted. It would seem that Troy would want to be vastly different from his father, but it is not within his power to rearrange fate. He sees the other woman and "got to thinking that if I tried . . . I just might be able to steal second" [70], have a marital affair without family disruption.

When Troy's wife asks him, "Don't you think it ever crossed my mind to want to know other men?" [70], he becomes furious, grabbing her roughly by the arm. Their teenage son intervenes and receives the blow that would certainly have struck her had he not arrived on the scene. It is Lucy's verbal acuity that causes John to smack her. When he tries to downplay his affairs through rationalization, she levels him with a folkloric eloquence. "Big talk ain't changin' whut you doin'," she says, though she is about at the point of death. "You can't clean yo'self wid yo' tongue lak uh cat" [128–29]. When John strikes her in her condition, it is a testament to the strife many men undergo when confronted with the reality of women as equals.

Hurston is sympathetic with that difficulty because John had been one to proclaim, "Ah don't choose beatin' lady people. Uh man is crazy tuh do dat" [51]. Moreover, before John struck Lucy, Hattie had gone to An' Dangie Dewoe to have a curse put on John, an event that would seem trivial but for the fact that Hurston perceived some voodoo practices as being as viable as any of the more orthodox religions. Shortly after the publication of *Gourd*

Vine, she received two consecutive Guggenheim fellowships to pursue research on this very subject, research that would culminate in the fascinating volume, *Tell My Horse: Voodoo and Life in Haiti and Jamaica* (1938). It is of the utmost importance that John may have been influenced by voodoo. By introducing the voodoo element, Hurston has added an ambiguity along the lines of what we will find in *Their Eyes* when Janie kills Tea Cake in self-defense. Ravaged by rabies, he points a gun at her and begins pulling the trigger. She has just enough time to fire back before his shot hits her. Janie has rid herself of the "fiend in him." Previously, Tea Cake had struck her because it "reassured him in possession." Recall he had been inclined to disappear for extended periods, more than likely engaging in "extra-marital" affairs. Those factors would have been enough for Janie to have wanted retribution. Yet Hurston raises the scenario to a different level – the ultimate one of life and death – where the survival of woman is at stake. Man is the threat, and Hurston has arranged for his elimination as such.

Yet, the irreconcilable fact remains that Tea Cake had rabies and, in the literal sense, was not in control of his faculties. Nor can we say that John has control over his own actions in those situations where he has resorted to beating women. After Lucy dies, he marries Hattie and "beat her whenever she vexed him." Was he under a voodoo spell? How does Hurston want us to assess this man who is now trapped in a spiraling decline?

Hurston biographer Lillie Howard submits that "John sees himself as a Christ figure throughout most of the novel" [87]. Clearly, by the time John gives his "The Wounds of Jesus" sermon we can draw an analogy between Christ's sufferings and those of the preacher. John directs the congregation:

> Notice at de supper table
> As He gazed upon His friends, ha!
> His eyes flowin' wid tears, ha! He said
> "My soul is exceedingly sorrowful unto death, ha!
> For this night, ha!
> One of you shall betray me, ha!
> It were not a Roman officer, ha!
> It were not a centurion
> But one of you [177].

Christ was betrayed by one of his own disciples; John is betrayed by none other than a member of his own deacon board. Conspiring with Hattie, Deacon Harris urges her to file for divorce because "mos' of the folks whut would stand up for Rev'und so hard, is gone" and "de time done come when we kin chop down dis Jonah's gourd vine" [154]. Instead of a Christ figure, John should be perceived as a mortal, but one who is entrusted with a divine mission.

Continuing the same sermon, John declares, "Wounded in the house of His friends. / That's where I got off de damnation train / And dat's where you must get off" [181]. Upon finishing that sermon, he resigns his pastorship of the church and thereby his fall from grace is complete. Swaggart had his "Benedict Arnold," Marvin Gorman, who turned telltale photographs over to the Assemblies of God. Jim Bakker had Jimmy Swaggart, who pushed charges that his PTL ("Praise the Lord" Club) rival had an affair with a secretary. Just one year prior to his own precipitous fall, Swaggart had labeled Baker "a cancer on the body of Christ." During that turbulent period in the late 1980s, religious hypocrisy was a prevailing theme of the day. The paradox becomes clearer as we consider how moral ineptness has consumed the very leaders who were supposed to be our moral stalwarts.

If we thought Deacon Harris wanted to get rid of John out of some sense of moral obligation to the congregation, then we are abruptly brought around to the harsh reality as Hurston informs us that the real reason Harris wants to bring John down is "to move the man who had taken his best side-girl from him" [159]. After marrying Hattie, John had continued his adulterous affairs; he was bound to infringe, sooner or later, on others' relationships. What is so startling is how Harris has reacted like any other jilted lover. He is not remorseful in his hypocrisy, but instead is intent on gaining vengeance. Seen in this light, he is no more or less than "every man."

A century earlier Nathaniel Hawthorne had perceived this universality of the human condition. In "Young Goodman Brown" (1835), not only Deacon Gookin but also Goody Cloyse, who taught catechisms, and the minister himself are convening with the Devil out in the secluded woods. After witnessing that evil meeting, Brown withdraws from the human community. He snatches children away from Goody and "when the minister spoke from the pulpit . . . then did Goodman Brown turn pale, dreading, lest the roof should thunder down upon the gray blasphemer and his hearers" [89]. He scowls now as the family kneels at prayer, and he "shrank from the bosom of Faith," who, in addition to being his wife, is the personification of belief in God. In rejecting the human community because of its hypocrisy, Brown becomes the epitomy of hopelessness. His response to the realization of hypocrisy has been to retreat and, even in death, there is no sense that salvation is possible.

Hurston is not so pessimistic. Or to put it another way, she did not believe that human feelings should eliminate any prospect for hope. When Jonah of the Old Testament wants the city of Nineveh to suffer the brunt of God's wrath, this prophet is disturbed that God decides to spare the city's inhabitants. Having fled the city, Jonah comes to Tarshish, where God makes a gourd vine suddenly spring up so the prophet can have relief from the sun. But almost as quickly as He provides the shady vine, He then destroys it, whereupon Jonah becomes resentful, mourning his loss and thereby revealing his own startling hypocrisy. God Himself, in Jonah 4:10–11, observes that the prophet "had pity on the gourd, for that which thou hast not laboured, neither madest it grow; which came up in a night, and perished in a night: And should not I spare Nineveh, that great city, wherein are more than sixscore thousand persons that cannot discern between their right hand and their left hand; and also much cattle?" A divine objectivity is conveyed through those words as God explains His decision to spare Nineveh. Yes, God caused the flood in Noah's day, but if He were to go around destroying populations every time he found sin, humankind would be quickly extinguished. Such hopelessness is not what He envisioned when He caused the flood. Otherwise He would never have had Noah build the ark to give humankind a second chance.

In Hurston's novel, John's second chance comes through Sally Lovelace, who is the epitomy of what her last name implies and offers him an unconditional love that leads her to share with him the proceeds of rent from thirty houses. She shares everything with him, trusts him explicitly, and urges that he return to the place of his downfall to show how well he has done since he left.

He has even acquired a new church in Plant City that is larger than the congregation he had in Sanford. Moreover, he has found a way to be faithful; he vows "never tuh sleep uh night" away from her. Of course, that vow is broken when she insists that he pay a return visit to Sanford. Sally does not understand the nature of temptation as it pertains to John. Once back in Sanford, he is no match for the plump Ora Patton, who with her "big, good-looking daddy" and "pretty, curly headed man" entreaties will seduce him into a back room. Sally never does learn of his infidelity. "He sho wuz true tuh me," she consoles herself after John's death. The author has spared the widow's feelings, but left us in a quandary about how we should interpret the final state of affairs.

I would disagree with what Rita Dove says in her foreword to the 1990 edition. She accuses Hurston of having "a little too much local color." That critic, furthermore, questions the apparent need Hurston saw for including sustained elements of folklore to the point where entire sermons are excerpted for use. Dove argues that such blocks of folkloric "fieldwork" detract from the overall quality of the novel, "interrupting the narrative flow." The critic is particularly concerned that the train imagery used by Hurston in "The Wounds of Jesus" sermon "seems too heavy-handed a foreshadowing" of the death that John meets when a train kills him on his way back to Sally in Plant City.

Firstly, that sermon should not be viewed as interrupting the narrative flow. In fact, it was brilliantly placed by the artist. Just before John gives the sermon, he is at the point in his career where he is being utterly betrayed. He draws important parallels between his own life and what Jesus experienced in the matter of betrayal. After giving the sermon, John resigns his position to become an "ordinary" man, and we can evaluate him in terms of what Hurston's message might be with regard to most men. At John's funeral, the preacher delivers a eulogy on

> Death who gives a cloak to the man who walked naked in the world. . . .
> O-go-doe, the voice of Death – that promises nothing, that speaks with tears only, and of the past. . . . The preacher wiped his mouth in the final way and said, "He wuz uh man, and nobody knowed 'im but God," and it was ended in rhythm. With the drumming of the feet, and the mournful dance of the heads, in rhythm [202].

In effect, one sermon after another, Hurston raises the ultimate question of how much control we have over the manner in which we live our lives. How much is history and fate? How much the consequences of our own actions? In his own sermon, John had warned others to get "off de damnation train." He spoke of a "Judgment Convention" where "two trains of Time shall meet on de trestle / And wreck de burning axles of de unformed ether." Obviously, the folkloric element is retained, but here Hurston also gives us two dimensions of time that will, in the final analysis, be reconciled. Far from being too heavy-handed a foreshadowing of the moment when John will be struck by a train, his sermon is invaluable in terms of helping us understand how Hurston felt about the status of humankind in juxtaposition with the impending immortal unknown. Flawed though he may be, John is not without hope once he, aided by the metaphorical, folkloric train, has escaped the plight of being just "uh man."

Father Peace:
Obstructing the Quest
for a Self

In his study of black religious cults, Arthur Huff Fauset specifies four criteria that compel followers to join such organizations. Fauset notes a desire on the part of members to be closer to a supernatural being. Furthermore, he emphasizes "the personality of the leader, relief from physical and mental illness, and race consciousness" [76] as factors attracting people into the ranks of various cults, particularly those coming into prominence during the 1920s and 1930s. Fauset analyzes such movements as the Mount Sinai Holy Church of America, the Moorish Science Temple of America, and Bishop "Daddy" Grace's United House of Prayer for All People. In summarizing his views of those organizations, he speaks of them with high regard as "graduate churches" where people who had become disenchanted with orthodox Christianity could seek a "deeper insight" into the mysteries of evangelical religion.

Especially significant, for the purposes of my study, is Fauset's chapter on Father Divine's Peace Mission Movement. The following practices listed by Fauset were important elements of that organization:

There are no food taboos.
Intoxicants are strictly forbidden.

Dancing with members of the opposite sex is strictly forbidden.
Speaking in tongues is tolerated but not essential.
Business enterprises are encouraged.
Any display of racial intolerance is strictly forbidden [66].

I will want to provide commentary on most of these items in relationship to Paule Marshall's *Brown Girl, Brownstones*, in which the adolescent Selina Boyce is torn between the love she has for her happy-go-lucky father and the love she has for her mother, who has different ideas about how her family's struggle for success should be conducted. The mother, Silla Boyce, starts out as a maid determined to gain ownership of a brownstone house in Brooklyn. The father, Deighton Boyce, has dabbled in different ventures, but once he inherits land in his native Barbados, he resolves to return there and stake out a course for his family's future development.

One of the most climactic points in the novel occurs when Silla secretly wrests that land from her husband and sells it to further the achievement of her goal in the United States. Upon realizing what his wife has done, Deighton becomes distraught but then appears to recover somewhat. He never fully recovers psychologically, however. And then when he suffers a severe arm injury at the mattress factory where he works, the total of his circumstances becomes too much for him to handle and he thus has been made ripe for conversion into Father Peace's religious movement.

In *Brown Girl*, Marshall provides innumerable hints that the Father Peace character is a fictionalized version of Father Divine, who arrived in New York City in 1915 and proceeded to accumulate by the end of the 1930s, as historian Robert Weisbrot reports, savings in access of fifteen million dollars [6]. We get a fuller sense of the magnitude of his operation as Weisbrot continues:

> The Peace Mission became particularly well known for its aggressive efforts to desegregate all aspects of American society. The movement itself was among the very few interracial religious bodies in the nation. In the mid-thirties Divine sought to expand it into the most exclusive northern neighborhoods. Using white disciples as secret emissaries to circumvent restrictive housing covenants, he acquired homes, hotels, and beachfronts for his integrated following in areas long regarded as unthinkable for blacks to inhabit. By the late 1930s the Peace Mission

had acquired several dozen centers providing over 2,000 acres of choice property far from the city slums [6].

Weisbrot's book is a thoroughly uplifting portrayal of a man and movement. Indeed Divine did make what could be considered advancements in the area of racial integration. There is, for example, the photograph that Weisbrot has included of Father Divine in the formerly segregated Ulster County, New York, a place the religious leader renamed "The Promised Land" as he encouraged his black followers to settle there. Additional settlements were founded with Divine overseeing the entire extended enterprise. Is there any wonder that Deighton was impressed? W.E.B. Du Bois visited one of Divine's communes and commended it for its success at helping people in need. Furthermore, the Reverend Leon Sullivan, founder of the renowned Opportunities Industrialization Center (OIC), acknowledges that he is indebted to Divine for the ideas and methodology of the Peace Mission. In the midst of the Depression, Divine's organization supplied thousands of people with work and fed many more who otherwise would have gone hungry. All of this was done without government support. The Mission was the epitome of self-help as a means of providing survival mechanisms and thereby facilitating the development of self-esteem.

Divine was also beneficial in terms of instilling yet another type of pride. While "colored" magazines, with their cream-complexioned models, advertised hair straighteners and skin lighteners, Divine discouraged the use of such products. In a 1951 interview held with a "Miss C," Divine maintained: "Practically all of my true followers abstain from the use of cosmetics and the custom of straightening their hair, or anything of that sort. . . . Of course, everybody should use soap and water to wash their face and hands and hair . . . but to use it excessively unnecessarily, to try to make themselves altogether different from what they really are – my true followers do not do those things." Hearing Divine talk, one is somewhat reminded of other black leaders such as Marcus Garvey and Malcolm X for whom race pride was a prerequisite for racial development.

The name Father Peace is a thinly veiled play on Divine's organization – the Peace Mission. Moreover, one of Divine's favorite expressions was "Peace, it is truly wonderful," a refrain repeated often enough to persuade many followers that he was fully at peace with himself and the surrounding world. The leader's objective was to convince others that they, regardless of socioeconomic status, could be privy to the same peacefulness.

Before we make our final assessment, though, of the state of being at peace, it is apropos to consider the effect of that condition on Deighton. At one time an effervescent, happy-go-lucky man, upon his release from the hospital now has a haze over his eyes and "his whole body seemed as limp as that arm. All of him might have been sucked into the machine and crushed. And because he was so limp, he seemed quiet inside. A kind of dead peace hovered about him" [158]. This is the Deighton who previously had such a zest for life that he dreamed of and worked at achieving goals that varied from being an accountant to playing the trumpet like Louis Armstrong. But something has changed. He has gone all the way from being at one point a tireless dreamer to being simply in a state of peace. However wonderful that might appear to be on the surface, the stark reality of the situation is that Deighton is in the throes of a severe emotional decline.

In her autobiographical essay "From the Poets in the Kitchen," Marshall talks about her development as a child and how even at the age of eight, she was a voracious reader. Visiting the Macon Street Branch of the Brooklyn Public Library, she read books by Jane Austen, Zane Grey, and many others. Those authors were white, however, and as Marshall recalls, "I sensed a lack after a time. Something I couldn't quite define was missing" [10]. Then one day she "came across a book by someone called Paul Laurence Dunbar, and opening it I found the photograph of a wistful, sad-eyed poet who to my surprise was black" [10]. She was particularly struck by Dunbar's "Little Brown Baby." The following introductory lines convey its essential thrust:

> Little brown baby wif spa'klin' eyes,
>   Come to yo' pappy an' set on his knee.
> What you been doin', suh–makin' san' pies?
>   Look at dat bib–you's ez du'ty ez me.
> Look at dat mouf–dat's merlasses, I bet;
>   Come hyeah, Maria, an' wipe off his han's.

Bees gwine to ketch you an' eat you up yit,
Bein' so sticky an' sweet–goodness lan's!
Little brown baby wif spa'klin' eyes,
Who's pappy's darlin' an' who's pappy's chile?   [*Poems*, 214]

Marshall mentions that she at first had difficulty with the dialect. Moreover, in that poem, the little brown child of the father is a boy who is his "pappy's pa'dner an' playmate an' joy." One can assume that Dunbar was chauvinistic in his selection of a male to be the gender of "pappy's chile." The father dotes on him in anticipation of an even stronger future bond. By comparison, Deighton's only son died at an early age. Yet, that loss does not detract from the lessons about self-discovery that he instills in Selina.

It is significant that Deighton's son had a heart that "wasn't good." As the symbolic source from which love emanates, the heart would have been the means whereby the boy-child and his father could have had a bond comparable to the one expressed by Dunbar in his poem.

Evidently, Marshall did not want such a bond between father and son in *Brown Girl*. In her work, the bond would be between Deighton and his daughter. So intent is Marshall on rendering this particular depiction that she raises in our minds the very serious question of whether or not Deighton was responsible for his son's death. Silla tells a friend, "The wuthless father had to take him out in a piece of old car and shake up his insides so it near kill him" [30]. Why would the father do this? Does he not know the extent of his son's delicate condition? However we might answer those questions, it is clear that a key authorial purpose has been served by the son's elimination.

In that essay where she talks about first reading "Little Brown Baby," Marshall remembers: "The poems spoke to me as nothing I had read before of the closeness, the special relationship I had had with my father, who by then had become an ardent believer in Father Divine and gone to live in Father's 'kingdom' in Harlem. Reading it helped to ease somewhat the tight knot of sorrow and longing I carried around in my chest that refused to go away" [10]. Again we are made to focus on the heart area of the body and what that part of the anatomy signifies. For the artist, it did not matter that her father was male and she was female. The bond between her father and herself could not have been any stronger. In *Brown Girl*, the son is eliminated to make this very point, that a male offspring's devotion could not have been more profound than what Selina brought to the union between herself and her father.

When Deighton learns that he has inherited land in Barbados, Selina is the first person he tells, confiding: "Don't broadcast it to the Sammy-cow-and-Duppy but my sister that just dead leave me piece of ground. Now how's that for news?" [12]. He tells his daughter before he tells his wife, knowing that he and that daughter share similar yearnings of the spirit. In bragging about how this land is so fertile that it can grow any type of crop and predicting how he and his family can now own a fabulous house "just like the white people," he expresses sentiments not totally unlike those of Silla, who wants to own a home in Brooklyn. Yet, Marshall accents the allegiance between Deighton and Selina. The daughter tells Silla that she, like her father, wants to live in Barbados. And when Selina overhears Silla clandestinely planning to sell the inherited land, the daughter warns her father: "She's gonna sell it. She's gonna sell it all. . . . She swore to Iris Hurley and Florrie Trotman that she's gonna sell the land. Your land" [86]. Deighton does not believe Silla has the power to achieve such an aim, so he does not worry and confidently assures Selina, "There's not a thing she can do" [87]. But Silla does accomplish exactly what she sets out to do with Deighton's property, undermining his dream in the process.

Leela Kapai, in evaluating dominant themes in the works of Paule Marshall, has concluded that the quest for identity is extremely important. *Brown Girl* is a quintessential bildungsroman, charting the development of Selina Boyce from the time when she is a girl on up to young adulthood. But as Kapai also observes, rather astutely, "There is no age when a sensitive soul has not been troubled by questions about the meaning of his very own existence and his relation to the world" [49]. Kapai furthermore stresses that specific minority groups "need more than ordinary effort to recognize and keep their identity alive" [49] in a mainstream society where minority concerns are not usually a priority. Indeed, those who are of Indo-European descent are more often encouraged to investigate their cultural backgrounds than are individuals whose forebears hailed from Africa or the Caribbean.

In a 1980 interview with Alexis DeVeaux, Marshall praised inhabitants of the Bournehills section of a fictional Caribbean island which is the setting for her second novel, *The Chosen Place, the Timeless People* (1969). Generation after generation of Bournehills natives resisted social change. A mulatto lawyer from the island's privileged classes gives this example of how the masses rejected Westernization:

> "There was the housing scheme government built with the help of that Canadian company. . . . Those people refused to go near it. Decent houses now with water run in and a proper toilet. They preferred the old shacks they live in. Why? Hear them" – and he suddenly lapsed into the strong island accent, parodying it – "'Because it's we house and we land'" [56].

The rejection of such modernization might seem ludicrous until one observes how intent Marshall is upon exposing the ways in which – long after the end of formal Caribbean slavery – Canada, England, and the United States found alternative ways to take advantage of human and material resources. New industry and foreign tourism present what is only a different means of exploiting the island's lower classes. While the Canadian-supported housing scheme appears on its surface to have been the brainchild of an altruistic foreign nation, we can be assured of one thing, that beneath the surface of that scheme lay the mechanism for foreign control and the only long-term interests being advanced were those of the seemingly beneficent Canadians.

As exploited as many of the natives are, Marshall insists they are not stupid. "They know," the author stated in her interview with DeVeaux, "that until a people, an oppressed people, have actually wrested power from their oppressors they cannot really come into their own" [124]. Marshall is a first-generation American whose parents were from Barbados. That Caribbean connection has been a strong enough feature in her psyche so that she has been inclined to investigate the circumstances of various real and fictional islands in each of her novels as a means of celebrating the strength of the human spirit. She looks to Barbados as a source for inspiration as she portrays both those who remained behind to resist the oppression and those who left in search of a better life in another land.

Historian Hilary Beckles has characterized Barbados as a nation where "the persistent struggle for social equality, civil rights and material betterment by blacks, coloureds and some whites, constitutes the central current which flows through the island's history since 1627" [xiv], when the first English settlers arrived and then quickly acquired a handful of African slaves. Indeed, as Beckles depicts the history from that time until so-called independence in 1966, it reads like a chronology of one uprising after another. Marshall uses one such revolt when she gives to the people of Bournehills a mythical version of the actual rebellion that was led by an African-born slave named Cuffee. Beckles describes that revolt:

> In May, 1675, a fully fledged plot by slaves to overthrow the planters and seize control of the island was unearthed by the militia. Governor Atkins noted that aborted revolt interrupted all public affairs. His investigative committee suggested that the organisers of the revolt were almost exclusively Coromantee men.... Slaves from other ethnic groups were also involved, and it was almost totally an affair of African-born slaves.
>
> The revolt was not spontaneous.... The rebels had been planning the insurrection for about three years.... It was not limited to any one parish or group of slaves, but was an islandwide conspiracy. Obtaining freedom by force of arms was the first objective. After they had seized control of the island, the rebels intended to establish an Asante-style monarchy under Cuffee, who was described as an "Ancient Gold Coast Negro" [37–38].

Marshall has made good use of that historical event as the Bournehills natives regularly commemorate Ned Cuffee and his efforts to capture Pyre Hill, where he and his fellow rebels "lived for almost three years like the maroons of Jamaica and bush Negroes of Guiana—free, at peace, dependent only on themselves, a nation apart" [287]. The Cuffee of *Chosen Place* legend was eventually captured and executed, bringing the uprising to an end in a fashion similar to that portrayed by Beckles, who notes the "random execution of the so-called leaders" [38]. Still, a crucial spark was ignited as Cuffee, in death, became a symbol of what can be accomplished when freedom is the primary goal.

Broadening the perspective of *Chosen Place* in a manner that Marshall surely would have approved, Eugenia Collier asserts that "the real protagonist" of *Chosen Place* "is the community of

Bournehills" instead of one particular person. She further analyzes that the island as a whole "seems in its geographical position to link the New World with Africa; it seems the center of the triangular trade" [307]. For Marshall, Bourne Island is the powerful cultural link between Africa and America, just as her own Barbadian parents were cultural reservoirs for her. Those parents had been agents in what Kapai referred to as the "more than ordinary effort" needed by minorities to shape their identities through utilizing the vestiges of generations past.

The same theme resonates in Marshall's most recent novel, *Daughters* (1991), where we have Ursa Mackenzie struggling with a past made all the more complex by the fact that her father is a Caribbean native (albeit one who will rise rapidly through the class ranks), while her mother was born in Connecticut. The Caribbean island this time is called Triunion, fictional and yet symbolic of the theoretical merging of African, Caribbean, and African American cultures. As with *Chosen Place*, the author has focused in her latest novel on the need for revolutionary change so that the peasant class of Triunion can break free from the shackles of a colonialism that continues to bind them even after their presumed transition into national independence. The "Do-Nothing" native government is just an offspring of English rule, and as Ursa's mother phrases it in a letter home to Connecticut, "the old gang is still entrenched" [170], making it virtually impossible to invoke the much-needed reform.

In *Chosen Place*, Cuffee served as the inspiration with his insurrectionary efforts to put an end to slavery. The comparable legend in *Daughters* involves "two coleaders, coconspirators, lovers, consorts, friends: he, Will Cudjoe, a cutlass in one hand, a stolen musket in the other and a bandage made of the finest Alencon lace around his head; she, Congo Jane, also doubly armed and wearing draped around her shoulders, the ends crisscrossing her chest like bandoliers, the shawl – Jane's famous shawl – that had supplied the bandage for the gunshot wound on Will Cudjoe's forehead" [138]. As had been the case with Cuffee, these two insurrectionists stage a formidable slave revolt. They will ultimately be killed, but not before infusing others with the spirit for revolutionary change. The Bournehills natives have their annual celebration where they reenact Cuffee's revolt. Similarly, the natives

of Triunion have built a monument to commemorate Congo Jane
and Will Cudjoe, but "instead of its being in town where everyone
could see it," the political party in power "stuck it all the way up
. . . in Morlands, so as not to offend the white people in town"
[140]. Marshall is making a profound point with her depiction of
where the statue is built. The aim of those in power is to appear
facilitative of positive social change. But in actuality, freedom for
the masses of Caribbean natives is not what the leaders have in
mind.

All the way back to her days as an undergraduate student, it
had been Ursa's intention to research and write about Congo Jane
and Will Cudjoe. As a graduating senior, the student chooses this
subject for her thesis and proposes the project to Professor
Crowder:

> I'd really like to go ahead with the paper. It's a subject that genuinely
> interests me. I'm curious to know what relations were like between the
> slave man and woman. How did they get along? What was the nature
> of their social, sexual and family life? How did they feel about each
> other, treat each other? My theory is that in spite of the circumstances
> their relations were mainly positive [13].

Crowder rejects Ursa's proposal. But even more interesting is the
manner in which he refuses. He waits until only three weeks remain in the semester before he tells her no. Ursa is left with the
unenviable task of having to devise "another topic, write another
proposal . . . do the research and all the reading and write a sixty-
page paper" [14], all this in addition to the other work she has to
do in winding down her other classes and preparing for gradua-
tion.

Crowder cannot care less whether Ursa graduates. And he
"was known to be the most progressive-thinking member of the
small history/sociology department and the friendliest" [12], which
is why Ursa went to him with her proposal. Her sources were to
be "the slave narratives and oral histories, the old plantation
records, Aptheker, the Angela Davis article" [12]. These would
have been Ursa's "scholarly texts." What better sources could she
have than those stories from slaves who actually lived the experience, the records kept by plantation owners delineating the
monetary value of their human property, Herbert Aptheker's
study of slave revolts, and a modern-day "slave," Angela Davis,

who staged an historic revolt of her own? What possible reason can Crowder have to refuse? This is the question that Ursa cannot get out of "her mind struggling to understand, to get at the real reason for his no" [13]. Perhaps even liberal whites have biases that have been inculcated by society at large. Crowder becomes disoriented by the wording of Ursa's proposal. She is going to investigate the relations between slave men and slave women. More specifically, she is going to prove that "slavery, for all its horrors, was a time when black men and women had it together, were together, stood together" [94]. She has already learned that Congo Jane and Will Cudjoe cannot be evaluated separately. One cannot "call her name or his . . . without calling or at least thinking of the other, they had been so close" [94]. Such a prospect flies in the face of all the rationalizations that have been used to explain slavery and the various discriminations perpetuated long after the formal institution has itself been dismantled. In spite of the physical and psychological brutality that they had undergone, slaves and their immediate descendants retained their humanity and in doing so proved themselves to be much greater exemplars of humanness than those who would insist on the social subjugation of black people. This is the reality that Crowder prefers to keep hidden. Indeed it is so important that it not be revealed, that he is prepared to see Ursa eliminated from academia. For him, her personal survival is not so important as is the perpetuation of the myth that allows whites to believe their societal development is the product of a morally viable enterprise.

One of the reasons Marshall was not as critical of Father Divine as she might have been is that he did offer blacks an option that neither mainstream America nor the traditional black church was providing. It is important to note, as Weisbrot has pointed out, that Divine was "known for attracting many former disciples of Marcus Garvey, the premier black separatist figure of an earlier era" [190]. Garvey had founded the Universal Negro Improvement Association in his native Jamaica in 1914, and he opened his first United States office in New York City two years later. The principal aim of the UNIA had been to transport blacks back to Africa. The assumption was that absolute equality between the races could never be achieved in America.

What was it exactly that attracted former Garveyites to Divine? To put it succinctly, the organizations of each of these two men appealed to the people's hunger for independence and their need for self-esteem. Garvey had started the Black Star Line Corporation and encouraged his followers to invest in that venture, even though many could afford only meager investments. Yet ordinary blacks were being included in what had the makings of an extraordinary enterprise. By the same token, Divine stood at the helm of a monumental commercial venture with a seemingly unending number of branches where blacks could become actively involved. Weisbrot conveys the staggering details:

> The Peace Mission was easily among the most impressive examples of cooperative enterprise in the nation. By the mid-1930s the Peace Mission had become the largest realty holder in Harlem, with three apartment houses, nine private houses, fifteen to twenty flats, and several meetings halls with dormitories on the upper floors. In addition, followers in Harlem operated some twenty-five restaurants, six groceries, ten barber shops, ten cleaning stores, two dozen huckster wagons with clams and oysters or fresh vegetables, and a coal business with three trucks ranging from Harlem to the mines in Pennsylvania [122–23].

The diversity of functions is phenomenal, but we must at the same time consider how Divine may have exploited workers both for their money and labor. I will furthermore want to show why Marshall was so concerned about the psychological effects of such an organization on individual members. For the time being, however, consider the enormous appeal such a movement must have had for many blacks who heretofore had been excluded from such commercial activity. As Weisbrot points out, "Father Divine saw no contradiction between a spiritual calling and an economic reward" [124]. Evidently, few of his followers saw a need to make that distinction either.

Divine exhorted his followers to have confidence in themselves and their individual abilities. He was able to convince them that God created every individual for a specific purpose and that it was paramount for each person to work at ascertaining that purpose. In this regard, Divine was not unlike Marshall's Father Peace who proclaims: "Individual freedom is something glorious to attain for only then can you be truly one with God. Be wholly independent. God's conception and nobody else's" [168]. Marshall can appreciate that admonition, for her writing is in some ways a therapeutic exercise meant to reconcile insufficiencies in terms of how she perceived herself when she was a girl. In the interview with DeVeaux, she explained:

> In my writing I am always dealing from a base that happens to be me. It is, frankly, a means by which I can deal with aspects of my own personal history. I am both Black American and West Indian and, by ancestry, African. The West Indies is so very important to me because it is part of a history that as a girl growing up in Brooklyn, going to school with those heavy silver bangles on my wrists, and when we went back to the West Indies and came back with heavy West Indian accents, the kids used to laugh at us. It was dreadful. So I went through a whole period of rejecting that part of myself [123–24].

We can understand how the author must have empathized with Selina's father, who seeks psychological refuge in a return to Barbados. Deighton seeks empowerment through his Caribbean heritage. When this plan is thwarted, he turns to Father Peace, who, through his form of spiritual advocacy, anesthetizes Deighton, while appearing to offer a constructive option.

Weisbrot draws our attention to the fact that those West Indians who became Divinites were "generally from the darker-skinned and least affluent strata of their native societies" [61]. We have seen in *Quicksand* how Helga's light skin is an inducement for Pleasant to marry her. It is apropos to consider how intra- and interracial color consciousness influences interpersonal perspectives in general, regardless of the particular region or country. Whether it was during the time when Noah cursed Ham, or when Hitler "cursed" the Jews, or when the Americas carried out their enslavement of blacks, skin hue was a factor that facilitated the process. The phenomenon can be viewed in contemporary times as we witness, for example, the disparity between how Haitian and Vietnamese refugees are treated upon their arrival on United States shores. The difference in treatment is based to a large extent on the difference in skin color. Respect is rationed out in proportion to how close in appearance one is to the Nordic model.

Dark-skinned Barbadians living in America during the Great Depression suffered an intense form of discrimination, outcast from mainstream white America and also kept at a distance by many African Americans, who viewed them as different and inferior. So when the Peace Mission opened its door to West Indians and did so ostensibly under an all-encompassing umbrella of equality, quite a few West Indians jumped at the opportunity. And then there were the Peace Mission banquets. Selina asks her father to take her to see Father Peace; she wants to see who this man is who has consumed so much of her father's attention. When she gets to the place where Father Peace is, it turns out to be a brownstone in which "there were no walls but only one long high room, garishly lighted and filled with the festal sound of voices and eating" [164]. In this room is a long banquet table at which every seat is taken while a throng of other people stand waiting for the first group to finish so that they, in turn, can find a place at the table. "There was no wine and wafer here. The body of this god," Selina observes, "was large platters of fricassee chicken, roast duck, spareribs and big bowls of clogged rice; his blood, pitchers of milk and imitation-flavored soft drinks" [164]. The very fact that Marshall uses the lower case for the first letter of the word *god* gives us some indication of how she regards the religious ritual. It is not coincidental that at the same time Deighton is contemplating joining Peace's commune, Selina's older sister Ina "suddenly joined" the St. Matthew's Episcopal Church. Ina is the one who calls Deighton's plan to return home "nothing but silly dreams." She has no creativity or sense of her own worth; she needs the support of a god, and one might imagine that almost any god will do. She is like Deighton, who himself has become a "shadow" with his substance "irretrievably lost."

Instead of altars, flowers, and holy statues, banquets were the symbols of Divine's ministry. Contrary to the biblical admonition against gluttony, he encouraged his followers to eat abundantly without ever fasting or eliminating certain foods from their diet. The banquet was, in essence, an attractive recruiting technique, especially during the Depression, but also for any time people were caught in dire straights. No money was demanded on those occasions. It was widely known that if you were poor you could eat without expense. Others gave fifteen cents or whatever they felt was appropriate and could afford. The banquets were not where Divine reaped his fortune. That would be obtained by other methods.

Still, there was even a trick to the banquets. Relying on the observations of banquet visitors uncommitted to Divine's organization, Weisbrot explains:

> Rather than serve all food at once, he had waitresses first bring out pitchers of water, tea, and other beverages while he poured coffee for the guests. All were encouraged to drink freely while talking and singing hymns. Only after much time had elapsed did the first solid food appear – mainly starches and perhaps some fruits and vegetables. By the time the meats arrived, visitors had pretty much filled up on the preceding, less expensive portions of the menu. The roasts passed back and forth impressively across the table, then were reclaimed fairly intact, to be frozen for future use [36].

That tactic allowed Divine to get the most out of his food supplies; however, it should not be ignored that many supplies were nevertheless needed to feed the tens of thousands of people who lived at and visited his communes. At least fifty-five different dishes were served at every meal, and as Weisbrot puts it, "The tale of Jesus feeding the multitudes scarcely seemed more miraculous to Peace Mission members than their own awesome feasts, huge enough to have converted every Pharisee in Galilee, or to convince thousands in the nation's most frightful slums that Father Divine was truly God on earth" [81]. These banquets certainly were comparable, as far as many of Divine's followers were concerned, to what the biblical John reports as Christ's converting of "five barley loaves and two small fishes" (John 6:9) into enough food to feed five thousand people. Christ's act was the evidence that He was the Son of God. For members of the Peace Mission, Divine was the incarnation of God Himself.

Taking her place in turn at the banquet table, Selina sits beside an old woman, who suddenly throws up her arms and shouts, "Beautiful, beautiful Father! I knowed he's God. I knowed it" [165]. The woman goes on to testify that when she was sick and bedridden, "Father came" after the doctors had given up on her. Such testimony is not all that unusual at religious meetings of any denomination. In more recent times, Oral Roberts of Tulsa, Oklahoma has made faith-healing a vital part of his services. But what made Father Peace so unique was how he, in the eyes of his followers, went beyond being merely an agent of God to the point where he was accepted as the deity.

Joseph Washington, in his study of black sects and cults, elaborates on Divine's "seventy-five heavens," which were actually the religious communes through which he profited, although he demanded no regular offering at his services or any fees for his enormous banquets. Fauset, with his tendency to be deferential in his analysis of the Peace Mission Movement, professes: "No collections of any kind are ever taken at a Father Divine Peace Mission Movement service. Undoubtedly huge sums of money are required to carry on the work of the movement, but I have no information in regard to the source of these funds" [60]. Yet Fauset provides us with an answer to the very question for which he purports to have no answer when he describes

> two types of members. A great many members merely subscribe to the beliefs and practices of the cult, but otherwise live their lives normally as citizens of their community....
> The other type of member ... has renounced the things of this world completely.... If he is the possessor of worldly goods, he disposes of them in a manner agreed upon between him and the leader. He does not choose his own vocation or business, but places himself at the disposition of the Father.... Literally everything which such a member receives, the bread he eats, the raiment he wears, his lodging and work, whatever personal remuneration he may receive, comes through the direction of Father Divine. Such members are the true angels of the cult [60].

The nature of these two options becomes crystallized even further in Ruth Boaz's 1965 *Ebony* magazine article. She had, only two years earlier, defected from the movement in which she was once a fervent believer. In the article, she discredits any claim that Divine might have had to the higher calling of religious advocacy. "I now know that he is a charlatan," Boaz contends, "who has turned the fears and frustrations of countless unhappy people to his own profit" [89]. Boaz had been experiencing various difficulties in her life when she was targeted for recruitment into the movement. Once she did become a member, she devoted herself to what she then perceived as Divine's spiritual purpose; she ardently believed he was the "savior of mankind." Her perspective gained greater clarity after thirty years of membership, however, two years of which were spent as Divine's confidential secretary.

Of the second type of Peace Mission member, the one who renounced all the "things of this world," Fauset said that such a person disposed of worldly goods in a manner agreed upon between that member and Divine. When it came to the matter of membership and financial resources, however, Fauset was quick to add that that issue could be answered "only as a result of a rather long experience as a member of the cult" [60]. In Boaz we have such a former member, who details more starkly the two categories of membership which Fauset describes. According to Boaz, those in the "renounced worldly goods" category, once in the movement, had absolutely no control over their possessions. Those whom Fauset refers to as "true angels" are called by Boaz "consecrated followers," who were "expected to give up all his or her worldly possessions, convert property to cash and 'donate' everything to Father. Once the money is turned over it is never seen again. Nor may consecrated followers inquire about how much money they have donated or what happened to it" [94]. If we can believe Boaz, then we must assume that these consecrated followers had no power over their own lives, but had to abide unstintingly by Divine's wishes.

Boaz also gives information on the first of Fauset's two types of Peace Mission members. Even if not a resident in one of Divine's communes, a follower, Boaz explains, could "enjoy consecrated status even if he works at non–Kingdom jobs providing he donates generously to the movement" [95]. With such a stipulation placed on their religious status, one wonders how "normally," to use Fauset's word, such members lived their lives "as citizens of their community." Many of the members in both categories were subject to what amounted to an emotional slavery. They were the quasi-slaves; Divine was their master.

One of the goals that Divine had for his followers was that they deny traditional family ties. Marshall effectively portrays this aspect of the movement when at the banquet table, Peace admonishes, "The word *mother* is a filthy word. When a person reaches God he cannot permit an earthly wife or so-called children to lead him away" [168–69]. It would seem that Peace has put his own addendum to Christ's instruction in Matthew 19:14 to "suffer little children, and forbid them not, to come unto me." The disciples had pushed the children toward the back of the crowd, but Jesus preferred instead that they come to the front so He could "lay hands on" them. For the Son of God, children were an unquestionable priority. For Peace and Divine, children were nuisances not to be endured unless they "came unto him" (the cult leader, that is) and forsook any previous family relationships. Marshall was greatly disturbed by that feature of the organization. As mentioned earlier, the author, as a child, had an identity crisis. She obviously developed into an astute and highly capable adult, and she has such a development in mind for Selina. But as the normally perceptive Selina listens to Peace expound on the conditions for membership, "she was no longer wise or old, but confounded by life still" [169]. There is the potential for regression along the lines of what psychiatrists Lauretta Bender and M.A. Spalding uncovered in their study of children whose parents were followers of Divine.

These psychiatrists observed that "Father Divine is the family life, he is both mother and father of the parents and children. The children call their mother big sister and their father big brother" [460]. Among the case studies used for their article "Behavior Problems in Children from the Homes of Followers of Father Divine" (1940) are two quite revealing situations, both involving boys, one nine years old and the other twelve. At the time of the study, the first boy was himself a member of the Peace Mission. Bender and Spalding refer to him as a "child of superior intelligence." They came into contact with him, however, because he was brought into court by his own mother, who felt she could no longer control him. Among his transgressions were stealing and playing hookey from school. But upon further analysis it becomes clear that the child stole money to attend the movies and skipped school in order to play with other children. It seems his mother disallowed both of those social activities which any normal child would have wanted to be involved in.

Throughout Bender and Spalding's examinations of this otherwise superior child, his responses were extremely disconcerting. The authors convey, "He stated that his mother was not his real mother and that Father Divine was both his mother and his father" [463]. As far as that boy was concerned, the only way that babies could be conceived was "by committing adultery." Consequently, according to his distorted reasoning, the process whereby he came into the world was an unreconcilable sin.

When asked whether or not he had any regrets about not having a father, in the sense that other boys and girls have one, the respondent retorted, "I have one. Father Divine." What is most revealing, however, is that at a psychiatric session conducted one week after that reply, he confided "that he was hungry for his mother's love, that he had been deprived of it and that he would like to have his mother call him her child and not her brother" [463]. The interviewers noted that he showed "great anxiety," fearing that Divine might somehow get knowledge of his confession and kill him as a consequence.

Fear, as Boaz stated, was at the heart of Divine's methods for control. The twelve-year-old boy of the Bender and Spalding study was deserted by both parents, who went off to live in separate Peace Mission facilities. That child was one of five offspring the couple had, but he turned out the worst, going back and forth between an aunt and his mother, whose religion forbade her to take care of him. By the time he came under psychiatric observation, he had failed two grades and taken to the streets, where his residence became a variety of dark hallways. Needless to say, the court recommended that he be placed in foster care, where he might begin to recover from the circumstances that led him to believe as a rationalization for his parents' actions, that "Divine puts something in the food and drink that makes people 'crazy, 'cause they never acted that way before'" [467].

And then on the other hand, that second boy's explanation may have been more than just a rationalization. Further clinical studies substantiate the view that certain Peace Mission members were prone to strange behavior.

Bender joined yet another psychiatrist, Zuleika Yarrell, in a study of eighteen Divinites who had been admitted to the Bellevue Psychopathic Hospital in New York City. In the resulting article, "Psychoses Among Followers of Father Divine" (1938), patients conveyed the details of having suffered delusions and hallucinations. One patient recalled:

> I tried to stay away but something seemed to draw me back yet I know I didn't like the place. . . . I could not understand how God's work could make people such lunatics. I tried to keep away from the place and then it seemed hypnotic power came over me. . . . I got frightened and went to the police station for help [427].

Another patient drew the following conclusions about Divine:

> He studied the mind and he has power over people. He puts these spells
> on people.... I can hear his voice in me. He tries to control me in every
> way. I hear him everywhere [436].

In characterizing the types of people who join cults, Fauset mentions that they are likely to be seeking relief from emotional or physical anguish. One wonders what such individuals' states of mind were at learning that the man to whom they had been so devoted was not God at all, but just a man with a talent for exploiting people in dire need.

Deighton has studied accounting extensively, but because of racial discrimination, he is unable to attain suitable employment in that field. This factor, combined with the arm injury and loss of his land, makes him a prime candidate for Peace's cult. In her article, Boaz tells of her first encounter with Divine, how she and her mother visited his Sayville, Long Island, headquarters upon a member's invitation and how indeed that first meeting was a lavish banquet. Divine had made preparations for Boaz in particular. The author recalled that even in the midst of a large gathering: "He knew we were there and motioned for us to take designated places at the table. I was given the seat of honor which had been occupied by one of his favored white secretaries" [92]. Later in this chapter, I will elaborate further on the significance of race as it pertains to Divine's secretaries and other members of his movement. For the moment, however, I wish to linger on the preparedness of Divine at the arrival of a potential new member.

In *Brown Girl*, Marshall emphasizes this state of preparedness. At the banquet he attends with Selina, Deighton begins to focus on Peace's forefinger, which "was crooked invitingly in his direction, beckoning Deighton with a slow hypnotic motion" [166]. Most of the diners are more in tune with what is happening, while Deighton must be prompted: "Go on, Brother, Father's recognizing *you* tonight! Go on! [167]. As was the case with Boaz, he is offered a place of honor beside the cult leader. Deighton "pitched forward," "stumbled forward," and was "drawn it seemed by an invisible thread pulled by Father's finger" [167]. We will discover later that while seated beside Peace, Deighton was asked to live in a Peace Mission facility. He will become one of the consecrated followers who works out his life in that organization for room and board as his only material remuneration. Boaz speaks of being summoned by Divine to one of his private offices. Suspecting that she was disenchanted with life, "he leaned over and said tenderly: 'You can tell me *everything*'" [92]. Once she confided in him, he was able to use that information to his best advantage. By comparison, Deighton has certain accounting skills that Peace seems to have found out about because he makes Deighton manager of a peace restaurant. Silla must now work longer hours to compensate for her husband's lack of financial support, and his daughters feel the pain of his desertion. At the banquet, Selina thinks back to

> Percy Challenor presiding like a threatening god at the head of his table on Sundays. They were alike, he and Father Peace. They ruled. What was it that made her father unfit to do the same? Why was he the seduced follower and not the god...? [169]

The ellipsis marks are Marshall's, intended to convey Selina's extended meditation on this issue, a meditation that began four years earlier when she, at the age of eleven, visited her best friend, Beryl Challenor. Beryl's family was eating dinner when Selina arrived and was confronted with Beryl's domineering father, Percy. He was, in Selina's mind, "a pagan deity of wrath, his children the subjects cowering before the fire flaring from his nostrils, his wife the priestess ministering to his needs" [54]. Thus early in the novel Selina is confronted with the issue of how power is acquired and maintained.

In one sense this matter of power retention has to do with the nature of a male-dominated world. Men are paid more than women for doing comparable work. Men control the vast majority of social, political, and industrial institutions. And even within the sphere of family life, it is the man who is head of the household in those instances where he is present at all.

Race, on the other hand, is also a vital factor. Andrew Hacker, for example, has used an abundance of statistics in order to be persuasive in this vein. In everything from employment patterns to life expectancy, blacks rank significantly lower than whites, which leads Hacker to conclude:

So America may be seen as two separate nations. Of course, there are places where the races mingle. Yet in most significant respects, the separation is pervasive and penetrating. As a social and human division, it surpasses all others – even gender – in intensity and subordination [3].

Hacker argues that blacks in general have been subordinated in American society. One can look back to slavery for the origins of the discrimination and class delineations that have developed and persisted over the previous four centuries. But I would suggest that, particularly in recent years, race relations have fluctuated, often depending upon the economic condition of the country. Hacker concedes that indeed there are places where the races mingle. We might use that as a test to determine how much power blacks have acquired. Moreover, while the black lower classes have been unduly expanding, the black middle and upper-middle classes have been expanding as well. In many localities, blacks form the majorities on city councils and many blacks are mayors. How should we assess their access to or lack of power? Racism still exists, but is race still the biggest factor with regard to differentiating between those who have power and those to whom power is denied?

Trudier Harris characterizes Silla as having "accepted the tenets of the American Dream to the point of exploitation of people and, though she may sympathize with them, she is so intent upon retaining the power she has acquired that it is impossible for her to give total sway to her conscience" [66]. Father Peace has already been compared to Percy Challenor, who sits at the head of his own "banquet" table, the dictatorial leader of his family clan. Percy Challenor started off like Deighton, working in a mattress factory. But Percy is also a striver who sells stockings at night in order to make payments on two mortgages. He will eventually make his fortune in real estate, amassing so much property that one could say he has a kingdom.

In one of the appendixes of Kenneth Burnham's book *God Comes to America* (1979), there is a list of Divine's real estate holdings at the time that he moved to Philadelphia in 1942. The properties include churches, training schools, farms, hotels, and other extensions and cooperatives valued in the hundreds of millions of dollars. The leader was known to proclaim from time to time that he had "mastered the economic situation." The moral issue, however, has to do with exactly how he was able to master the economic situation and – as Harris implies in the case of Silla – to what extent his conscience had to be ignored.

Just as was the case with Divine, Peace, and Percy, Silla has her own version of the banquet table. She is the dominant conversationalist among a group of West Indian women immigrants who work from early morning to midafternoon as maids for well-to-do Jewish families. After work they gather in Silla's basement kitchen to discuss the day's events and offer moral support to one another. In the autobiographical essay "From the Poets in the Kitchen," Marshall pays tribute to the cultural eloquence of their language and acknowledges that they were more important as "literary" models than the classic writers she read. She was strongly influenced by certain classic writers, but those writers, says Marshall, "were preceded in my life by another set of giants whom I always acknowledge before all others: the group of women around the table long ago. They taught me my first lessons in the narrative art" [12]. In Marshall's novel, Silla is the master at such a table, mixing standard English and African sounds with metaphors, parables, and biblical quotations to create a distinct language style.

But Silla displays much more than just style in her use of language. She also displays profound substance. She is another striver, prodding her associates to take the Machiavellian approach to tackling life:

> People got to make their own way. And nearly always to make your way ... you got to be hard and sometimes misuse others, even your own.... Power is a thing that don really have nothing to do with color. Look how white people had little children their own color working in coal mines and sweatshops years back. Look how those whelps in Africa sold us for next skin to nothing.... Take this world. It wun always be white. No, mahn. It gon be somebody else turn soon.... And when they get up top they might not be so nice either, 'cause power is a thing don make you nice.... What's that saying 'bout the race is not to the swift? ... I tell yuh, you *best be* swift, if not somebody come and trample you quick enough [224–25].

Silla remains determined to become a homeowner. She joins the exclusive Association of Barbadian Homeowners, which Selina will come to regard as the epitomy of "living by the most shameful codes possible – dog eat dog, exploitation, the strong over the weak" [227]. But Selina's views do not stop Silla from living by those codes. The mother who had been a maid will struggle to get and keep a job at a defense factory. She makes further plans, taking a course in practical nursing. She already has two boarders, but when she decides on a plan to convert their quarters into more rooms to be rented out at higher rates, she quickly gets rid of one woman – ostensibly because of the company she keeps – and kills the other, an elderly woman, by torturously upbraiding her on the matter of cleanliness. Silla will eventually get the money she needs in order to buy the brownstone, but at what human cost? Harris argues that Silla is a "driven capitalist," who "continues to give up something of her humanity" [66–67]. In this regard she is quite tragic in spite of her material acquisition.

For all of Percy's hard-earned accomplishments, he too falls far short of any humanitarian ideal. Selina had thought when she saw him at his Sunday dinner that "he was too big to live among ordinary people" [54]. He has told his daughter Beryl to be a lawyer because "you can always make money at that among your own people" [59]. He is aware of the need for lawyers among those who have not gained equal protection under the law. I do not get the sense, however, that he wants Beryl to help ameliorate unjust conditions so much as he wants her to exploit the situation for her own monetary gain.

Percy believes that a career in law will be for Beryl a ploy virtually guaranteeing success. One of Peace's ploys, in addition to his call for peace and brotherhood for all humanity, is *The New Light* periodical that Deighton has been reading constantly since he was hospitalized. Once back home "he read only those newspapers and nothing beyond their pages seemed important" [160]. Before going to live on the premises of the peace restaurant, he spends his days in the sun parlor reading and rereading the issues of this newspaper. When he eats, it is "with *The New Light* propped against his plate" [160]. It has gotten to the point that he can stare at Selina for extended periods of time without even realizing who she is. He merely murmurs, "Peace, it's truly wonderful," "Thank you, Father," or just the word "wonderful" over and over again as though in a trance.

As she approaches young adulthood, Selina falls in love with an artist who resembles in many ways how her father had been before his capitulation to Peace's movement. That boyfriend, Clive Springer, understands how difficult it is to be individualistic. Such a perspective on life can be scary, but the alternative, as he expresses it, is at least as frightening. Commenting on the psychological makeup of the members of the Association of Barbadian Homeowners, Springer says: "Most people want to be one with the lowing herd, to be told, to be led. They gladly hand over themselves to something" [264]. While Springer is talking about the homeowners association, Selina makes the connection between the types of people who join that group and those who join Peace's movement. She remembers how absolutely alone her father had seemed when he appeared at a social function dominated by homeowners association members. After enough setbacks he had been psychologically primed for the Peace organization.

Listening to Springer, she remembers "with the old ache her father's head bent in ecstasy and immolation on the huge banquet table" [264]. Rather than eternal life, as Divine promised his followers, Deighton has succumbed to a spiritual death, and most phenomenal of all, he has found a way to enjoy his anesthesized condition.

Marshall is sympathetic with those like Deighton who have fallen into the abyss. Merle Kinbona, the author's moral conscience in *Chosen Place*, detests how the people in power on Bourne Island have been able to keep the Bournehills natives in submission. "The church and the rumshop!" she insists. "They're one and the same. . . . Both a damn conspiracy to keep us pacified and in ignorance" [133]. It is rather daring to assert that the church is no better at curing social ills than an alcoholic beverage establishment. But the author was not hesitant to utter that refrain. Before Merle spoke the words, it had been Silla who declared:

> The rum shop and the church join together to keep we pacify and in ignorance. It's a terrible thing to know that you gon be poor all yuh life, no matter how hard you work. You does stop trying after a time. People does see you so and call you lazy. But it ain laziness. It just that you does give up. You does kind of die inside [70].

Of course, Silla will never give up on her dreams. Just as was the case with the author's own mother, she will persist in her struggle for an intermediary goal and then pass the torch on to her daughter. Yet Silla vindicates those who are unable to muster the kind of intestinal fortitude that she herself possesses. She understands their frustration and perceives how they are the perfect prey for any force with a slick enough formula for control.

In the early stages of his career, Father Divine found it advantageous to keep the details of his origins obscure. He was born George Baker, probably in 1877 or 1883. But he routinely stated that he got married in 1882, a date that would push his birthdate back to the time of the Civil War. He died in 1965, so it is conceivable that he lived to be over one hundred years old, which would be an unusual feat in itself.

Baker worked his way up from the Deep South to Baltimore by 1899, and he earned his living there by clipping hedges and mowing lawns. During that same time, he taught Sunday School and attended Wednesday evening prayer meetings at a black Baptist church. During those Wednesday evening sessions, Baker would rise to given informal sermons. Weisbrot notes, "Baker quickly gained favor with his fellow congregants, who shouted encouraging amens and 'Brother, ain't it so!' throughout his messages" [16]. Those sessions must have fostered a great deal of confidence in Baker, who continued to seek avenues for his sermonic expressions.

New York City would prove to be the setting for Baker's rise through the ranks of religious practitioners, but his acquisition of fame was not immediate. Calling himself first Major J. Devine and then the Reverend Major J. Divine, he would enter by 1919 into a crucial phase with his purchase of a spacious home in the all-white community of Sayville. Worshipers flocked to his elaborate Sunday banquets, causing whites in the community to resent his presence not so much because of the noise factor associated with his services as because of the threat Divine posed to the unwritten rules against racial integration. Whites ate and worshiped with blacks at Divine's Sayville mansion. It was particularly bothersome to white community leaders that among Divine's worshipers were white women who accepted Divine as their savior.

Judge Lewis J. Smith encompassed in his persona an accumulation of all the fears that Sayville residents had concerning Divine infiltrating their neighborhood. Officially accused of disturbing the peace, the cult leader appeared before this judge who, in spite of the jury's recommendation for leniency, gave him the maximum possible sentence of one year in jail and a fine of five hundred dollars. Divine accepted his fate with a considerable amount of poise, so much poise in fact that when Smith suddenly keeled over and died three days later, there were many who believed that Divine himself had exacted revenge against Smith for the mockery of a trial that the judge had conducted.

While there is no evidence that the cult leader ever claimed to have killed Smith, his silence on the matter at times and phrases along the lines of "I hated to do it" at other times were his attempts to capitalize on the bizarre turn of events. Shortly after Smith's death, Divine was released on bail, and when the case came up on appeal, the unconscionable verdict was overturned. In the final analysis, Divine received justice. The year was 1933; blacks were still being lynched in various parts of the country. Divine fought the system, however, and won in convincing style, providing, in some people's estimations, further evidence that he was God.

Deighton is swayed by that chain of events, convinced as others are that Peace has the power to hurt those who stand in his way. Fauset interviewed a follower who told of a voter registration clerk who refused to register Divinites under the new names they had assumed since joining the movement. That follower, Sing Happy, reported how Divine confronted the clerk, admonishing him: "You must obey the law. You must register my people" [54]. The clerk refused, and according to the interviewee, within half an hour the clerk died of a heart attack. Was this coincidence? Did the interviewee tell the story the way it really happened? However one might answer these questions, it must be conceded that the perpetuation of one such story after another would make almost anyone at least wonder if Divine's religious claims had some merit.

On one particular day, Selina holds Deighton's framed photograph of Peace in her hands as she ponders "his hold over her father." She gradually becomes infuriated and shakes the picture

until the glass drops out of the frame and breaks. Before hitting
the floor, the glass cuts her on her arm. When Deighton arrives
and sees what has happened, his beliefs are reaffirmed. He is "ex-
ultant," almost as a child would be, and takes the opportunity to
harangue Selina on the topic that was in every Divinite's argu-
mentative arsenal:

> You see? You see? Father struck you down! You interfere with him and
> he struck you down! . . . Go ahead, keep interfering and he gon strike
> you down each time. Just like he does all them who interfere with him
> and refuse to believe he's God. Take that big-shot Judge Jones. He put
> Father in jail. And Father prophesy that he was gon die the next day.
> And he die! . . . He die, I tell you, that big-shot white judge die . . . and
> the big-shot white doctors cun tell what he die from. You think Father
> was frighten for them 'cause they was white? Not Father. He let loose
> his power and showed them he's God Incarnate [162–63].

Marshall substituted the name "Jones" for that of Smith who was
the judge at Divine's trial. But the author's allusion is only thinly
veiled, because she has substituted one very common name for
another very common name, protecting herself against slander
while nevertheless allowing the extraordinary circumstances to
maintain their historical proportions.

Another name that is very effective for Marshall's purposes
is "Peace" itself. This name is perhaps even more effective than
the name "Divine," since it might be claimed that what everybody
wants, by a certain point in life, is to find solace in the midst of
difficult circumstances. This is what Father Peace presumes to
offer. One can only hope to be able to overcome any obstacles that
might interfere with the attainment of that goal. In Peace's case,
a major obstacle is Judge Jones, who is in a larger sense the universal threat to tranquility that we all have to face in some form
or another. Peace wins his joust with the "demon," but not everyone can single-handedly secure such a victory. Consequently,
there will be those willing to submit themselves totally to someone who reigns as a battle-tested entity.

The circumstances surrounding the death of Judge Jones
provide added incentive for Deighton to espouse the tenets of
Peace's organization, the most significant one for Selina being the
fact that he is willing to desert her and the rest of his family. And
yet, one wonders exactly why Peace and Divine insisted upon this

requirement. On the surface, the logic is understandable. A husband with his wife and children would all be brothers and sisters
within the framework of the movement to make it clearer who the
real leader was. The head of the Peace Movement did not want
internal threats to his power.

But beyond that organizational demand, there lurks the psychological makings of something even more sinister. Relying on
various independent claims, Weisbrot raises the prospect that
long before he became Father Divine, this cult leader deserted his
own family. Since Divine wanted his followers to believe he was
God, he tried to keep his past a mystery, and he was largely successful in this endeavor. He encouraged cult members to believe
that he just materialized from thin air to pursue his worldly mission. But what if he did desert his family? From a psychological
perspective, how likely is it that he would have wanted to nourish
others in their desires to keep their families intact?

Furthermore, it strikes me as hypocritical that while members of his movement were denied their otherwise legitimate
right to maintain traditional family ties, Divine himself could
marry whenever he chose. One of his disciples, an older woman
named Pinninnah, was at first simply a valuable assistant because
she made significant financial contributions. Her name, along
with Divine's, appeared on the deed of sale for the Sayville property. She was almost as mysterious as the leader himself, and it
is uncertain whether she was an associate of Divine's from his
early days in the South or whether she joined him after his arrival
in the North. Whichever was the case, by 1919 she was recognized
as Father Divine's wife, and shortly thereafter her title was se-
cured. She would be Mother Divine.

When that first Mother Divine died in 1937, the cult leader
avoided informing his followers for fear of exposing a contradiction. The movement had promised eternal life to those who were
faithful to the cause. Heaven was not something to be reached
later. It was a state of being, right here on earth. So instead of
immediately having to explain her death, Divine left the matter
as a mere disappearance from public view on her part. No one
dared ask questions openly. Not, that is, until he married again
in 1946, this time to a twenty-one-year-old white woman he barely
knew. Of course, the interracial aspect of the marriage gained

national media attention, but even within the movement, questions arose with regard to his choice of a newcomer who was white and so young and with regard to his violation of his own rule forbidding marriage. Perhaps Divine could simply have reminded them that he was God and not subject to the same behavioral stipulations that were really designed for the masses.

But the leader was not quite that brazen, at least in his public statements. Instead, as Weisbrot asserts, "Divine assured his followers that his was not a marriage in the conventional sense but a spiritual union to symbolize interracial harmony and uphold a standard of chaste conduct for others in the movement" [214]. Divine presented this union as one that had never been consummated through sexual intercourse. Still, Boaz, the woman who had been his confidential secretary, insists that he could be deceptive in the way he wanted himself perceived by the public at large. She reveals that the leader actually refused some proffered gifts of large estates, and he dramatically declined to accept donations from people outside the organization. The aim was to present himself as a man who took nothing for himself but merely gave. His banquet sessions fueled this perception. Meanwhile, declares Boaz, he secretly collected millions of dollars from his consecrated followers.

Charting Divine's cooperative-style kingdom from the early 1930s until the last years of his life, Boaz provides an even more in-depth view of the inner workings of his empire:

> Until Father became ill the followers usually paid their money directly to him. . . . Money was usually given to Father during his interviewing hours. For years the outside co-workers paid their tribute to Father Divine either on pay day or on their day off. Father directed that all donations be put in envelopes. By Divine decree the interviews at which donations were given were not to exceed five seconds. . . .
> All the co-workers who perform duties inside the Peace Mission movement – waitresses, cooks, chambermaids, chauffeurs, housekeepers, secretaries, etc. – must sign contracts which state that they are working voluntarily and will never ask any compensation for services rendered [95–96].

The procedure for "outside co-worker" payments must have served a dual function. Five seconds was such a short period of time that once the money changed hands there was little chance of tracing names and amounts of money given to the leader. At the same time, members had the opportunity to speak, albeit briefly, with God. Anyone who has ever sat in a church pew and experienced the pressure to give that members of a congregation indirectly apply on one another can imagine the degree of coercion involved when the money must be put in the deity's hand.

After having been relieved of her "inside co-worker" secretarial responsibilities, Boaz spent the next twenty years working off and on as a maid and nurse. "During those years," she states in the *Ebony* article, she "earned an estimated $75,000, at least $50,000 of which I gave to Father Divine. I gave as little as $10 a week and as much as $1,000 at a time. No receipt was ever issued and no record ever made of these payments" [96]. Deighton likewise is an "inside co-worker" whose labor relegates him to the status of an indentured servant, if not a virtual slave.

Boaz initially believed, like so many others, that the cult leader was God and as such was entitled to privileges not necessarily allowed to others. He, for example, could marry a second Mother Divine and declare it to have been for the purpose of upholding "a standard of chaste conduct for others" [Weisbrot 214]. But Boaz reached her limit of tolerance at the point where, as she attests, Divine made "physical love" to her and then explained, "When I have sex relations with you I am bringing your desire to the surface so that I can eliminate it. God is the only one who can do as he pleases" [92]. Here we witness the prerogative of so-called divine privilege. But the ludicrousness of Divine's rationalization process proves that the leader was mired in his own contradictions. While engagement in sexual intercourse does appease the sexual urge, it does not eliminate it indefinitely.

Another contradiction becomes apparent upon a closer analysis of Mission ceremonies. In analyzing the banquet, Marshall emphasizes the actions of certain white women. Weisbrot notes that "the extremes of ardent behavior at these banquets occurred mainly among certain women followers but still cut across racial and class lines" [86]. It is important to note that Weisbrot's subtitle is "The Struggle for Racial Equality," and he is mainly interested in portraying Divine as a black leader who made significant social contributions. Indeed Divine insisted that blacks and whites sit in integrated fashion at those banquets, and he mandated that whites had to lodge with blacks in his cooperatives. Further-more, his organization could take credit for integrating many pre-viously all-white suburban neighborhoods. Weisbrot downplays a vital psychological reality, however, as he ignores the phenome-non of white Divinites being accorded more respect in the move-ment than the masses of blacks who nonetheless formed Divine's main support base.

In *Brown Girl*, when Peace advocates total freedom for his followers, it is quite interesting that the person who most visibly responds to his entreaty is a young woman who "stretched her white arms to him," proclaiming, "I love you, Father! . . . I love you" [168]. At the same time, the crowd has been whipped into an almost uncontrollable frenzy that does not dissipate until

> a young white woman stood up, lifted her face, and the tumult subsided a little. "Father Peace is the perfect expression of God," she said quietly, her face like a Madonna's, her blond hair falling in a golden cowl on her shoulders. "Outside in the world there is immorality, and the things that come of immorality: wars and ambition, hate and carnal lust. The way people live out there is death. Here is only happiness and immor-tality with Father! Oh, you're so beautiful, Father dear. Your words are beautiful. They are fit company for your beautiful little face and body. . . ." She smiled sweetly at him and he gave her a pleased nod, and the others might have vanished and left them alone with their love [166].

Compare that to how black women are described with their "caved-in" and "work-ruined" faces, and we have the subtle sym-bolism of a racial hierarchy within the Peace Mission itself.

Weisbrot acknowledges the "disproportion of white disciples holding positions of responsibility," but he justifies it as "a policy of awarding positions based solely on education and professional certification that naturally favored the largely white middle-class element in the movement" [77]. With his access to such wide-spread financial and human resources, one wonders why Divine did not initiate a barrage of schools and training centers to help alleviate some of the societal inadequacy with regard to the mat-ter of education. Considering how his influence spanned several decades, he might have greatly altered the hierarchical structure of at least his own organization.

Evidence would suggest that this was not his major aim. Absolute independence was not what he desired for the masses. Instead, what he sought was a way to exploit their condition and give advantages only to the extent that such development did not lessen his control. One way of explaining why the Madonna-like woman is the announcer at the banquet in *Brown Girl* is to assess the advertisement practices of American enterprises in general. Many companies and other organizations use attractive white women to sell their products. These women are put out front, and the public responds to their presence.

Divine must have been conscious of what Stember has called the "value of a Caucasian appearance." This is an alternative way of explaining why whites dominated the upper levels of his organizational hierarchy. As much as he may have wished to seem egalitarian when it came to racial matters and as concerned as he was about black pride, he was not free of the psychological consequences of living in a culture where white women, for untold generations, were placed on a pedestal. This would explain the need for a white Mother Divine. It further explains his attraction to Boaz, whose status nonetheless was diminished when "a new, attractive, younger secretary was added to the staff and Father turned his attention to her" [92]. One wonders if the new secretary was white also.

Whatever the race of Divine's new secretary, it is clear that Marshall wants us to view Peace as a man willing to engage in profound compromise. It is a syndrome acceded to by those who acquire power. Marshall expounds on the phenomenon in brilliant artistic fashion in *Daughters*, where she has two black men rise from their humble origins, one in Triunion and the other in the appropriately named American city of Midland. The peasant blacks of Triunion regularly vote for Primus Mackenzie, who they assume is fighting for their interests because he is black and from their economically depressed community. Instead, he engages in questionable behavior, committing adultery, for example, and ultimately looking out primarily for his own best interests and the interests of those who have money. All the while, he is passing himself off as a man concerned about the natives, that poverty-stricken group from which he had evolved.

Back in Midland, Sandy Lawson has risen from his humble beginnings to become mayor, yet not much improves for the black underclass which spawned him. His world is now defined by "tall stately windows with their drapes, the polished brass chandeliers and the paneled walls to the side hung with any number of plaques, citations and photographs" [282]. Mackenzie had been concerned with the building of roads and hotels for the convenience of tourists who frequented the island. Mayor Lawson is concerned about completing a highway that will allow white suburbanites easier access to their jobs in the inner city. Both of these prominent political leaders assume that the black masses will continue to be supportive, regardless of the fact that they received virtually nothing for their votes. Marshall resolves part of the dilemma by having Mackenzie finally voted out of office. Lawson seems headed for a similar downfall as Mae Ryland, representing the grassroots of Midland's black population, vows, "If we see he just ain't no *use* no kinda way, we'll vote his little gap-toothed self outta there the same way we voted him in, and find us another. . . . And if that one don't do right neither, we'll vote his butt out too, and just keep on till we find us the right one. The right one's got to be out there somewheres" [299]. The black Midland community will continue to seek resolution by searching within the bounds of American shores.

At the end of *Brown Girl*, however, Marshall suggests something quite different. In a rather ambiguous moment, Selina removes one of two bangles (presumably representative of her Barbadian heritage) from her wrist and tosses it to the rubble of what had formerly been the brownstones, that symbol of Barbadian immigrant aspiration. The city is about to use the site for a new housing project, and Selina will leave, as Eugenia Collier has suggested, "to begin her travels, probably starting with Barbados" [303]. Collier believes that by throwing away one of her bangles, Selina leaves "something of her self behind" [303]. Perhaps so. But more importantly, Selina, through this act, is acknowledging the limitations of her American experience. She will journey now to Barbados and probably Africa, as well, to learn firsthand of her ancestral roots and thereby acquire the means to create a self free from "New World" manipulators.

From the Hypocrisy of the Reverend Woods to Mama Day's Faith of the Spirit

In the "Dawn" section that begins *The Women of Brewster Place*, our attention is drawn to a housing project that "became especially fond of its colored daughters as they milled like determined spirits among its decay, trying to make it a home" [4]. Prior to the slow but steady arrival of these black women, the premises had been inhabited first by Irish immigrants and then by "dark haired and mellow-skinned" Mediterraneans. The women of Brewster Place are the last in a long line of lower-class citizens who have struggled to rise above the socioeconomic barriers that often press new arrivals to this country down and inhibit their attempts to enter into the mainstream. These women are not new arrivals, however; they are the descendants of slaves brought to American shores untold generations ago. It is sometimes mindboggling to contemplate how, even today, most immigrants seem, in general, to fare better than African American counterparts who have been here so much longer.

What was the method by which blacks were so consistently left out? Of course, slavery itself was the biggest holdback. And then even after formal slavery ended, various forms of quasi-slavery – for example, sharecropping and Jim Crow laws – were instituted to perpetuate many of the conditions that had been the hallmark of the original slavery situation. Well into this twentieth century, black people as a social block were denied the opportunities that would have given them access to political and economic power. If blacks blamed white society for the predicament, they would not be entirely wrong. It is whites who have been in power from the earliest colonial days to the present. It is whites who initiated slavery as it has existed in this country. And whites, in many ways, have aided and abetted the perpetuation of racial distinctions that have almost always spelled inferior status for blacks.

Yet, particularly as we read *Brewster Place*, we must wonder about the extent to which blacks share complicity for their own degradation. Lucielia Louise Turner is largely responsible for the electrocution of Serena and the abortion of what would have been her second child. That mother made what turns out to be an unreliable man her priority over the care she might otherwise have given her children. That man, Eugene, selfishly comes and goes as he pleases, complaining, "With two kids and you on my back, I ain't never gonna have nothin'" [95]. So he can leave, and, upon returning, lie with regard to his whereabouts. He counts on Ciel to sympathize with him, and she does so until profound tragedy occurs. Confronted with the loss of his children, he simply leaves once again, not particularly caring whether Ciel will be able to recover emotionally.

Naylor claims to have done all she could to avoid black male bashing. In an interview with Toni Morrison, she insisted that in *Brewster Place* she had

> bent over backwards not to have a negative message come through about the men. My emotional energy was spent creating a woman's world, telling her side of it because I knew it hadn't been done enough in literature. But I worried about whether or not the problems that were being caused by the men in the women's lives would be interpreted as some bitter statement I had to make about black men ["Conversation," 579].

Perhaps the author's portrayals of problems caused by men were not intended to be a "bitter statement," but it cannot be denied that she is issuing a firm indictment. From the beginning of the novel, where Butch Fuller abdicates any responsibility for his part in the sexual liaison with Mattie Michael, to near the end, where C.C. Baker rapes Lorraine, we are given views of black men that run the gamut of interpersonal horrors.

Critic Larry Andrews has suggested that "most of the men in the novel may indeed be so ego-crippled by racism as to be unable to love their women" [10]. Such may be the case for Butch in pre–1960s Rock Vale, Tennessee, and for C.C. in his urban ghetto environment. But the Reverend Moreland T. Woods's psychological situation is quite different. He is not an ego-crippled black man. Naylor characterizes his congregation as a group of people who "would have followed him to do battle with the emperor of the world. . . . They would willingly give over half of their little to keep this man in comfort" [66]. In the minds of those followers, he is God's anointed representative. Although not as conspicuous as Divine in terms of wealth and prestige, he is nonetheless equally dangerous.

Manipulation is at the heart of Woods's intentions. On the night Etta Mae Johnson visits the church, "he glided to the podium with the effortlessness of a well-oiled machine. . . . He eyed the congregation confidently. . . . He was going to wrap his voice around their souls and squeeze until they screamed to be relieved" [65]. This preacher understands the nature of his power and knows how to use it for the greatest effect.

But Etta also had manipulative power. Previously she had finagled a Cadillac out of a married man who was in the delicate position of not even being able to report the theft since the sheriff was his wife's father and not likely to think kindly of an unfaithful son-in-law. That son-in-law was powerless, and Etta knew it. Obviously, she is adept at some of the vicious games that people are capable of playing with one another. So why is it that she has no chance of winning the game she plays with Moreland?

For the church service, she wears a scarlet dress that is "too little dress" revealing "too much bosom." She accomplishes through intention what Helga Crane inadvertently achieves when she dons her red dress and wanders into the storefront church in Harlem. Just as Pleasant had been attracted to Helga, Moreland "noticed Etta from the moment she'd entered the church. She stood out like a bright red bird among the drab morality that dried up the breasts and formed rolls around the stomachs of the other church sisters" [67]. Etta stands out not only because she exudes sexuality. She stands out through the sheer force of her distinct personality. While still a young girl in Rock Vale, she had acquired the name "Tut" because she "always had her chin thrust toward the horizon that came to mean everything Rock Vale did not" [59]. We have seen the word *horizon* used before as a means of portraying (im)possibility and woman. At the very beginning of *Their Eyes*, we are told that men's dreams "sail forever on the horizon" even if those wishes do not "come in with the tide" [9]. There is always some precedent in the world for men's aspirations, while women have no such advantage.

But Etta is unusual. There in Rock Vale, she "was not only unwilling to play by the rules," but she even goes so far as to challenge "the very right of the game to exist" [59]. She is a rebel who, though it is the 1930s, can look whites straight in the eye and treat them in accordance with what she thinks they deserve. Due to a set of rather ambiguous circumstances—in terms of their presentation in the novel—she is run out of Rutherford County. It has something to do with the tenuous situation of an interracial liaison. What we are told is that "she left one rainy summer night about three hours ahead of dawn and Johnny Brick's furious pursuing relatives" [60]. We are never actually told what Etta did to Johnny, but judging how those relatives "had waited in ambush for two days on the county line, and then had returned and burned down her father's barn" [60], it can be concluded that she retaliated violently to some kind of sexual indiscretion committed by Johnny. When we learn that "Etta was sorry she hadn't killed the horny white bastard," we can speculate further that what Johnny did was attempt to rape her.

Such were the circumstances of black life in the South. However, the issue becomes why Etta's life has not changed very much, even after her escape to the North. She remains a free spirit, but like Zora Hurston herself—who had to flee Eatonville to preserve her independence—Etta is an anomaly whose freedom of spirit is threatened by men who see women only as sex objects. Etta's situation is similar to that portrayed in Ann Petry's novel

The Street (1946), where men from every walk of life are obses-
sive in their efforts to seduce Lutie Johnson, who is attractive,
single, black, and poor.

One would think, though, that a minister would be different,
that instead of contributing to the oppression of black women,
Moreland would want to help them through their timeworn dilemma. As it turns out, however, he is not much different from
Hurston's Reverend Pearson in that they both are entangled in
a moral contradiction. While the Bible condemns fornication and
promiscuity, Moreland participates in those biblical offenses and
is still capable of rising into the pulpit to "damn into hell for the
rest of the congregation" the very life-style he himself is guilty of
practicing. He understands the nature of "the game" and is very
good at playing it. This is one reason why Etta, though excellent
herself at playing the game, has no chance of winning this time.

We get a vivid picture of the dynamics of male/female relationships as Naylor juxtaposes the societally presumed positions
of man versus woman within the metaphorical context of a card
game. Moreland, the preacher, becomes Moreland, the card
shark, who contemplates Etta and marvels

> how excellently she played the game.... And although she cut her
> cards with a reckless confidence, pushed her chips into the middle of
> the table as though the supply was unlimited, and could sit out the
> game until dawn, he knew. Oh, yes. Let her win a few, and then he
> would win just a few more, and she would be bankrupt long before the
> sun was up. And then there would be only one thing left to place on
> the table – and she would, because the stakes they were playing for
> were very high. But she was going to lose that last deal. She would lose
> because when she first sat down in that car she had everything riding
> on the fact that he didn't know the game existed [71–72].

The very name "Moreland Woods" should be a tip-off for us, particularly since we had seen how the name "Pleasant Green" was
an inadequate barometer for determining character. "Tea Cake
Woods," in *Their Eyes*, is one more deceptive name that, combined
with the other two, helps to convey the fact that men offer no
panacea for the predicament of women regardless of how respon-
sive those men might at first seem to be.

Inside the church, Moreland speaks with Etta for only a brief moment. If he takes any longer, the congregation will grow suspicious and assume he has ulterior motives with regard to the sultry visitor. "Just let me say good-bye to a few folks here," he tells Etta, "and I'll meet you outside" [69]. Mattie knows what Moreland has in mind; even Etta knows. Yet she also knows what the cards are that have been dealt to her as a woman. Moreland, with graying temples and gold-capped teeth, is no doubt older than Etta. But she is the one obsessed with the fear of growing old. Back in the "Mattie Michael" section of the novel, she had urged Mattie to go with her to New York City because of the "place called Harlem with nothing but wall-to-wall colored doctors and real estate men" [26]. Note that a woman as independent-minded as Etta is not going to New York to *become* a doctor or real estate agent. She goes to that metropolis with the intent to meet and marry a man in one of those two professions. As a child in Rock Vale, the reason she was called "Tut" had nothing to do with her appearing to others to have the power of a king. She was called "Tut" because one would have thought she was the "*wife* of King Tut" (my emphasis). The distinction is important even for a baby girl who, in that Southern village, had strutted "around . . . like a bantam." The diminutive aspect of the bantam breed of chicken refers not just to the fact that Etta was, at the time, small in stature. The author's use of the bantam is a reference to how any appearance of power that Etta exuded had to be weighed against the power of men and boys in the same community.

By the time Etta encounters Moreland, it has become abundantly clear that the reinforced values of society have caused the odds to be stacked heavily against her. She counts on the preacher not knowing just how delicate her position is as a lonely, single, middle-aged black woman. She misleads herself, but the author warns the reader of Moreland's "razor-thin instinct" and we are told that he is an "alert observer." Those traits are what facilitated his rise to the top of his theological profession. With Etta, he knows "exactly how much to give" [71] and how much he can take, and he knows that in the end she will submit to his sexual desires.

In analyzing Mattie and Etta, Barbara Christian concludes that they are both in Brewster Place "because of their concept of themselves as women. . . . These middle-aged women live through others" [356]. More specifically, they live through the men with whom their lives have become intertwined. It is an unquestionably profound revelation that for a woman like Etta, "even if someone had bothered to stop and tell her that the universe had expanded for her . . . she wouldn't have known how to shine alone" [60]. What this means is that even if those individualistic dreams flitting on the horizon were to become probable for her, she would not be in possession of what Christian calls the "psychological resources" to achieve those dreams without a "good" man by her side.

Naylor's message about such dependency is best conveyed as we look at how Moreland's treatment of Etta steadily deteriorates. In the early stages of their game, he "helped her into the front seat of his car" [71]. After the liaison is completed, he drops her off on a deserted avenue where she "got out of the car unassisted" [72]. In the midst of sexual intercourse, he beats "against her like a dying walrus" with his "floundering thrusts into her body" [72]. She is, for him, nothing more than a piece of meat primed for his sexual satisfaction. She was destined to be exploited in spite of her unique qualities, destined to be a pawn who will personify the struggle in which all the women of Brewster Place are engaged. Far from suggesting a solution, Moreland is a formidable obstruction intent on relegating women to a position where they will be no freer than the antebellum slave women who were vulnerable to being visited periodically by the master.

* * *

As we consider Naylor's second novel, *Linden Hills* (1985), it becomes clear that the problems prevalent in Brewster Place do not disappear just because some women have made it to an upper-middle-class neighborhood. The plight of Willa Prescott Nedeed exemplifies the circumstances of all the Nedeed wives. Willa has been cast off into the basement by her husband, Luther, who is the last in a long line of Nedeed men. Willa's offense is that she bore her husband a child who is too light-skinned.

In presenting the Nedeed family, Naylor has offered up another extreme case of male oppression, and yet as with the women in Brewster Place, we must ask to what extent the Nedeed women must bear some of the blame for their own predicaments.

It is Willa herself who wants to be a Nedeed. Her husband's distant predecessor was the founder of Linden Hills and within the framework of the black community, the Nedeeds have always wielded considerable power. As we are told:

> Her marriage to Luther Nedeed was her choice. . . . She knew then and now that there were no laws anywhere in this country that forced her to assume that name; she took it because she wanted to. . . . She must be clear about that before she went on to anything else: she wanted to be a Nedeed. After all, every literate person in the Western world knew it was a good name [278].

Even after she has been relegated to the basement, the power to emerge is in Willa's hands. She was "manipulated" down into that hole, but "she Willa Prescott Nedeed, had walked down twelve concrete steps. And since that was the truth – the pure, irreducible truth – whenever she was good and ready, she could walk back up" [280]. We are told – from a symbolic, surrealistic perspective – that her walk down those steps had begun "from the second she was born" [280]. She hears the deadbolt sliding into place, presumably locking her down there. Naylor wants us to understand that any attempt at progress under such conditions will be a difficult endeavor, but entirely possible once the requisite will-power is summoned.

Equally difficult, as Naylor presents it, is the more general struggle between good and evil. The author uses the Dantean concept of descending concentric circles to convey how as residents move down in Linden Hills to the more prestigious houses, they are inevitably "consumed" by Nedeed whose first name, incidentally, bears a striking resemblance to the name Lucifer, the Devil.

Over the course of the generations, what have the Luther Nedeeds (of each generation) been doing there at the bottom of Linden Hills? They have all been undertakers, specializing in what we can take to be more than the mere preparation of bodies for the grave. The Luthers deal in souls. When Winston Alcott forsakes his homosexual lover and instead marries a woman for the sake of appearances, there is a Luther of the Tupelo Realty Corporation who gives the newlywed couple a mortgage on Tupelo Drive, one of the lowest and most prestigious levels in Linden Hills. That same Luther has special praise for Lycentia Parker, who "spent her last days working" [135] in the effort to halt the construction of a housing project. It is not so important that she opposed the project. The point is that in opposing it, she joined forces with the Wayne County Citizens Alliance that, in young Willie Mason's words, "was the Ku Klux Klan without a Southern accent" [134]. What she has done, in effect, is plot with racist whites to prevent the less fortunate of her own race from having access to affordable housing.

But Lycentia is dead now, and in death she has become the object of a major confrontation between the Reverend Michael Hollis and Luther; the two men are literally in battle for that woman's soul. Luther wants her funeral services to be held in his own home, but Michael keeps control in this instance, insisting that the funeral "be held in his church and not some godforsaken funeral parlor if it was to be held at all" [165].

The nature of the battle becomes even more crystallized as we observe the home addresses of these two men. Luther's address is "999," which read upside down is the sign of the Devil. Michael's address is "000," which he argues: "aren't zeros, they're O's. Three eternal circles that are quite appropriate for a home owned by the church" [169]. According to the minister, the O's in his address signify the Holy Trinity. Michael further draws the distinction between himself and Luther by pointing out: "You could draw a straight line from my front door to Nedeed's down there at the bottom of that hill, there's a huge difference between how I earn my subsistence and how he does. Why, my life is devoted to the Lord and he's a. . . . Well, never mind" [170–71]. Like the Devil, who began as one of God's angels, Luther started out with good intentions. He was a real estate entrepreneur devoted to the advancement of blacks. But as he fostered that general prosperity, the economic achievement took precedence over spiritual salvation.

Michael serves as the human guardian who would prevent people from exchanging their souls for vast wealth. He warns Willie Mason:

> There are so many forces that govern our lives beyond the material, the tangible. There is to be an accounting, son, for each and every one of us. And we can't balance those books with our stock dividends. We better pay heed to that on this side, because when we get to the other

side and the body is gone, we might just find ourselves with no soul as well [169].

Even as he preaches, however, the reverend is in conflict with himself. Long before he came to Linden Hills, "he was twelve years old, sitting in the fifth row of his grandmother's weather-beaten church" with its "sagging walls miraculously held up by the Tennessee heat" [157]. A vital part of his past consisted of attending church in the rural South, where the services included "clapping and swaying" and every now and then "an unpredictable explosion of sound" [157]. That was the setting where he was "called" into the ministry.

It is quite telling that now Michael cannot remember what made him want to serve in a ministerial capacity. Despite his choice, "everyone knew that in four years Michael Hollis had never even made it to chapel" [159] when he was at the University of Pennsylvania. Although his reflections on the rural South are incomplete, he is, during his college years, still aware that "going to chapel wasn't" the same thing for him as "going to church." Church means to him something other than what was available to U-Penn's Sunday chapel. The distinction has to do with cultural roots, on the one hand, as opposed to the more sterilized version of religion that an Ivy League environment is likely to provide.

John Wideman, in his autobiographical *Brothers and Keepers* (1984), talks about having been on the verge of "coming apart" as a consequence of being one of "about ten of the seventeen hundred men and women who entered the University of Pennsylvania as freshmen in 1959" [29]. To maintain his equilibrium, he and another black freshman "would ride buses across Philly searching for places like home," and only after "a number of long, unsuccessful expeditions" did they finally find "South Street" [32]. Those two college classmates had searched for the poolrooms, barbershops, and rib joints that would remind them of their cultural origins and allow them to return to the university and endure that alien world.

Just as had been the case in real life with Wideman and his friend, Naylor's fictional preacher is able to find refuge in South Philadelphia.

On Sunday afternoons he quietly left the dorm and drove past the manicured lawn and Gothic stones of the Penn chapel into South Philadelphia to sit in the back of reconverted candy stores with stained-glass cellophane peeling at the windows. Where, more often than not, the altar was a scarred wooden table with an oilskin cloth and plastic crucifix; the battered piano missing keys if not pitch; the chairs missing leg braces if not backs.... Every Sunday ... Michael made the circuit: The Tabernacle of the Saints, The Zionist Mission, The House of Divine Ascension.... Sitting in the rear of those small rooms, he could almost see the currents racing from back to front and back again. The presence of that type of raw power connected up with something in his center [159].

While seated in the rear of those storefront churches, Michael is reunited with the raw energy he had felt as a child at the holy roller–type church service. He is reprieved momentarily, reenergized to the point where he can return to the campus and continue his academic studies.

Upon completing his undergraduate work, Michael enrolls at Harvard's divinity school while remaining committed to the style of worship that he learned in Tennessee. In Cambridge, he scorns "what Harvard considered a 'model sermon'" [161]. After graduating from the divinity school, he concludes that his degree is "total horse dung." As an undergraduate he made his way to South Philadelphia. As a graduate student he leaves the campus to attend Sunday services in Roxbury, where once again he can maintain his connection to the pulse of the common folk. He pursues Ivy League training but never loses sight of the source for his spiritual strength.

As he receives his pastorate in Linden Hills, Michael learns that he is about to be tested one more time. Unlike the down-to-earth congregations he has been affiliated with in the past, now his own congregation "stiffened under the cashmere, silk, and beaver skins, so he had to reach over them to the others, where he felt a supple willingness to receive, be filled, and return the energy he needed to keep going" [162]. The poorer members of his congregation sit in the back during church service, but he preaches over the pews of wealthy members to find those humble parishioners who are willing first to receive the spirit and then, by way of call-and-response technique, supply the verbal feedback to keep him inspired. But those seated up front with their "plastic postures" begin to consume more and more of the pews until Michael, in desperation, must resort to sponsoring Christmas parties specifically for the low-income neighborhood of Putney Wayne. Michael's object is to get Putney Wayne residents to attend Sinai Baptist on a regular basis. They come "at first, sitting in the back pews and the balconies, but gradually drifting away to where they could be free to worship as they believed" [163]. Thus Michael's source of strength disappears to the point where he becomes vulnerable and finally succumbs to the hedonistic life-style that he (like Moreland) nevertheless preaches against.

Catherine Ward renders this assessment of what the reverend's moral position has become after a sustained period in Linden Hills: "Years spent pursuing sensual pleasure and material possessions have isolated Hollis. He has an endless supply of women, closets full of expensive suits, and a couple of LTD's . . . and he has lost touch with his own feelings" [76]. He has slid into the world of strict materialism and fallen prey to that pervasive sin of adultery. He gets through his hypocritical days by periodically taking shots of Scotch and popping mints to cover the smell. At the critical juncture when he is faced with the task of preserving Lycentia's soul, we wonder how he can ever perform this particular mission.

"Are you ready for death?" [182] he asks those who have amassed for the funeral. Like a father confessor now himself confessing, he posits, "Will the fancy homes, fancy clothes, and fancy cars make you ready? Will the big bucks and big jobs make you ready?" [182]. Michael tells Lycentia's husband that Jesus is not ready to call his wife. If not now, then when? That is when Luther takes charge of the ceremony and recapitulates the events he regards as the highlights of her life, such as her work on the Linden Hills Beautification Project and her work as secretary of the Tupelo Realty's neighborhood board. Lycentia's "good works" helped raise the status of her community, consequently causing it to be separate from the lives of the masses of blacks.

Willie, symbolic of the masses, detects something devious in how Luther closes the lid of Lycentia's coffin:

> But he hadn't seen anything. Nothing but a man closing the lid of a coffin. And there was no harm in that. . . . A man leaning over and with

his hand closing the lid of a coffin.... It was that right hand. It moved too slowly over the top of the lid before it clicked shut ... it moved as if Nedeed was... [186].

Those last ellipses are another of the author's not so subtle hints that Luther is an agent of the Devil. It is he who will take authority over the dead body as though now collecting on the terms of some previous arrangement.

As we think back to Michael's explanation for the three "O's" in his street address, we recall what he said about the numbers representing the Holy Trinity. But after Luther takes charge, it seems more appropriate to consider how the numbers might suggest a negation. And as much as Michael's lifelong struggle has been to achieve a high level of spirituality, we must ultimately conclude he has failed in that endeavor. He is like one of T.S. Eliot's hollow men whose "dried voices ... are quiet and meaningless" [77]. While Luther is claiming authority, Michael "did absolutely nothing." Separated from the source of what has been his strength, he is drained of the spiritual essence that might have allowed him to defeat the proponents of evil.

* * *

In *Linden Hills* we are afforded a glimpse of the woman who in the author's next novel will come to symbolize what is needed for spiritual fulfillment. This essential woman is the great-aunt of Evelyn Creton, one of the Nedeed wives who remembers that as a child she had been "ashamed of her great-aunt, Miranda Day, when she pulled up in that cab each summer, calling from the curb at the top of her voice, 'Y'all better be home.'" [147]. The old woman was toothless, almost illiterate, and wore loose-fitting shoes. Evelyn shunned her so she would not be embarrassed in front of her teenage friends. Even then, the future Mrs. Nedeed was focused on social mobility, and Mama Day was proving to be a persistent inconvenience.

In the actual novel, *Mama Day* (1988), we are presented again with the dichotomy of material versus spiritual success. George Andrews has his own engineering firm and his job is "to redesign the structures that take care of our basic needs: water supply, heating, air conditioning, transportation" [60]. He is, quite simply, the mechanical man who is as detached from the spiritual realm as a person can get. However, his love interest is another of Mama Day's great-nieces, Ophelia, who while living in New York City is nonetheless torn between that impersonal venue and the island of Willow Springs, whose bridge connects it with the mainland right at the dividing line between South Carolina and Georgia. This is an important point because while both of those states have sought to usurp Willow Springs to be part of their individual territories, the island remains an entity unto itself with strong cultural ties to Africa.

That African connection is personified in legend through the person of the transported African, Sapphira, who married her owner, Bascombe Wade, bore him seven sons, arranged for Willow Springs to be deeded over to his slaves, and then killed him and walked right out onto the Atlantic Ocean, presumably en route back to her homeland. A similar occurrence can be seen in Toni Morrison's *Song of Solomon* (1977), where it is suggested that there were Africans brought to American shores who had the capacity to fly, if necessary, in order to return to the place of their origin. In both literary instances, we are confronted with an almost incomprehensible spirituality that is nevertheless used by the authors to criticize diluted forms of African American religiosity.

Paule Marshall's Avey Johnson (*Praisesong for the Widow,* 1983) is able only in retrospect to perceive that her and her husband's quest for the good life caused an emptiness that will not be remedied until she travels to the mysterious island of Carriacou. Similarly, Naylor's Ophelia must make the trip southward from New York City to achieve the dynamic spiritualism of her ancestral past. Mama Day lives in Willow Springs, and as an example of her powers, the author compares her to a medical doctor who is occasionally called to render services on the island. The physician, Brian Smithfield, is obliged to accept that there is

> no point in prescribing treatment for gout, bone inflammation, diabetes, or even heart trouble when the person's going straight to Miranda after seeing him for her yea or nay. And if it was nay, she'd send 'em right back to him with a list of reasons. Better to ask straight out how she been treating 'em and work around that. Although it hurt his pride at times, he'd admit inside it was usually no different than what he had to say himself – just plainer words and a slower cure than

them concentrated drugs. . . . Being a good doctor, he knew another one when he saw her [84].

These are serious ailments that Mama Day is at least as capable of handling as the degreed practitioner. In fact, hers is the final say-so even concerning prognoses that the doctor makes. A descendant of Sapphira, Mama Day carries on the tradition of that primordial ancestor who was indeed responsible for the Willow Springs community existing in the manner that it did with so much of its cultural essence intact.

Mama Day is, more specifically, a midwife. Literally speaking, that is her function for this community. But on a symbolic level, she is more. She serves as the source for spiritual creation and regeneration in the midst of an increasingly industrialized world. While the doctor's cures, for example, are condensed for mass consumption and institutionalized convenience, Mama Day tailors her remedies more precisely to the needs of her individual patients. Moreover, since she also functions in the realm of the spiritual, her powers far exceed the capabilities of those who are limited to practical means.

Houston Baker, in *Workings of the Spirit* (1991), points out "the importance conjure has historically possessed for an African diasporic community" [79]. In particular, Baker has reference to the fact that Zora Hurston was an initiate in a Louisiana hoodoo ceremony. The critic expands further on that intriguing phenomenon as he explains, "one reason the conjurer held such a powerful position in diasporic African communities, was her direct descent from the African medicine man and her place in a religion that had definable African antecedents" [79]. Mama Day is a prime example of how the fields of medicine and religion were so thoroughly intertwined in African culture. I would also add the field of politics as an arena in which the historic cultural figure of the conjurer played a role.

The revolutionary Ned Cuffee in Marshall's *Chosen Place* was an obeah man. Derived from the Ashanti word *obayifo*, *obeah* means capable of performing magic. Obviously, not everyone can lay claim to such power. But those who do, form part of a belief system where, as Roger Bastide reports in *African Civilizations in the New World* (1967), special individuals "fly through the air, suck the blood of their victims, radiate light from their anus, and turn themselves into animals" [103]. Childish superstition? Perhaps. But the mere fact that it is unexplainable is not enough to cause one to reject the possibility. Remember, Christianity itself is largely based on the acceptance of and faith in entities that are unseen and, for the practical person, totally unbelievable. Yet Christianity flourishes as one of the most pervasive modes of thought in the civilized world. Prior to the encroachment of Christianity on African soil, legitimate religious and political systems were already in place. As the wise Obierika explains in Chinua Achebe's *Things Fall Apart* (1959), "the white man is very clever. He came quietly and peaceably with his religion" [162]. But religion was only the beginning. By the end of that novel, we learn how introduction of a new religion has been the means whereby a foreign people has gained political control. "We have fallen apart" [162], mourns Obierika. Indeed, the cultural patterns have been seriously altered.

But ultimately the patterns are not destroyed. Resistance is as much a factor in Achebe's novel as is the European plot to usurp Nigerian authority. Resistance is also evident in the literature about blacks in the diaspora. Squire Gensir, in Claude McKay's *Banana Bottom* (1933), reminds those who would deny the validity of obeah practice:

> When you read in your stories about the Druids, the Greek and Roman gods . . . and the Nordic Odin, you felt tolerant about them. Didn't you? Then why should you be so intolerant about Obi and Obeahmen? . . . Obeah is part of your folklore, like your Anancy tales. . . . And your folklore is the spiritual link between you and your ancestral origin [125].

In that novel about Jamaica, white preachers use various methods of intimidation to steer the natives away from their own distinct religious practices and toward a belief in Christianity. Again we see how the attempt to gain religious sway is the preliminary step in the process of attaining general power over a presumed primitive community. Those descendants of Africans attend the Christian church, but then secretly at night they visit the Obeahman and thereby preserve their heritage.

Susan Willis has argued that the predominant theme of contemporary African American women writers is "the journey (both real and figural) back to the historical source of the black American community" [57]. We see this theory played out in Toni Morrison's *Beloved* (1987), where the former slave Baby Suggs, "accepting no title of honor before her name . . . became an unchurched preacher" who "opened her great heart to those who could use it" [87]. "Uncalled, unrobed, unanointed," her sanctuary is "the Clearing – a wide-open place cut deep in the woods nobody knew for what" [87]. Her tenure comes to an end only as the "big-city revivals" make their way out to the Clearing, which now is reached not by a simple, narrow pathway, but by a well-worn track signifying increased urbanization and a more formal, and thereby sterile, religious service.

Mama Day epitomizes a tradition similar to what Baby Suggs represents. The former has a supernatural understanding of her great-niece's needs and knows, for example, what type of man George is without having met him. She seems even to know of his general comings and goings without the benefit of engaging him in conversation. And of course she is gifted with the knowledge of an appropriate remedy when Ophelia is cursed by a woman who believes the great-niece is having an affair with her husband. George must facilitate the cure, and Mama Day orders him back to her own chicken coop in search of what lies beneath a formidable red hen. Mama Day insists, "You gotta take this book and cane in there with you, search good in the back of her nest, and come straight back here with whatever you find" [295]. There is nothing in the hen's nest. But nonetheless in that coop a vicious battle takes place between George, the harbinger of urban ideals, and the chicken, a symbol of the old ways, specifically as they pertain to African voodoo-type ceremonies. George succeeds in nullifying the curse, but he dies in the process. What he is able to accomplish is due only to the power of Mama Day.

This female conduit of African culture does more than offer her assistance in selected problem cases. She is the thread that holds together the Willow Springs community. We see this most profoundly as she orchestrates the yearly Candle Walk which takes place not on December 25, but on December 22. Naylor does not wish to eliminate Christian themes such as sacrifice and rebirth, but she does make it clear that Mama Day's celebration is not based on the Euro-centric approach to Christianity. There are legends associated with the Candle Walk ceremony, such as the one about the origin of Willow Springs, that "the island got spit out from the mouth of God, and when it fell to the earth it brought along an army of stars. He tried to reach down and scoop them back up, and found Himself shaking hands with the greatest conjure woman on earth" [110]. Is there any wonder why the old Reverend Hooper has tried his best to put an end to the Candle Walk ritual? From his perspective, the rite is sheer blasphemy. It cuts across the grain of biblical doctrine as it was imparted to him along the way toward his credentialed position.

On the other hand, that version of Willow Springs' origin can be viewed as a variation on the earth origin story presented within the first nineteen verses of Genesis. God remains the ultimate source of creation, but instead of the encounters the Old Testament describes with men such as Adam, Moses, Abraham, and David, this time the communion is with an empowered woman. Furthermore, there is the suggestion in *Mama Day* that God is a woman. Mama Day "goes to bed to get down on her stiffened knees and pray to the Father and Son as she'd been taught. But she falls asleep, murmuring the names of women" [280].

Much has been made over how gender references in the Bible denote God as a "him" or a "he." Moreover, Genesis 1:27 specifies that "God created man in his own image." Such details are enough to convince some people that God must be a man who correspondingly gave men on earth power far beyond anything that might have been afforded to women.

But as one reads on further in that Genesis verse, one finds the basis for some controversy. The passage continues, "In the image of God created he him; male and female created he them." Nowhere in the Bible are we given a physical description of God. That entity, spirit that it is, may defy gender classification. As we take this latter section of the verse in conjunction with the former, it seems more likely that the use of male gender in reference to God was as much for the sake of convenience as anything else.

What does it mean that the word "own" is emphasized in Genesis 1:27? Shug Avery, in *The Color Purple* (1982), offers Celie the following perspective:

The thing I believe. God is inside you and inside everybody else. You come into the world with God. But only them that search for it inside find it. And sometimes it just manifest itself even if you not looking, or don't know what you looking for. Trouble do it for most folks, I think. Sorrow, lord. Feeling like shit [202].

For black women to wait on a white male God for their redemption would be a ludicrous thing to even contemplate. Men, who have usually been the ones in control of biblical interpretations, have manipulated passages so that the world might be the way that they wished it to be. As one reanalyzes Genesis 1:27 in its entirety, it would seem that in creating both woman and man, God's intent was to have individuals be true to what was best in their own inner workings. The extent to which God pressed His image on them was only to inculcate morality.

It is important to note the time frame within which Mama Day prays and then unconsciously, in troubled sleep, murmurs women's names. It is when Ophelia is in the throes of the curse with her "eyes, lips, chin, forehead, and ears smeared everywhere, mashed in and wrinkled, with some gouged places still holding the imprints from [her] fingers." In a word, she has become an absolute monster with "flesh from both cheeks ... hanging in strings under [her] ears" [276]. That would certainly be enough to comprise the requisite "trouble" that Shug had in mind when she laid the conditions whereby God might be reached. It is in such dire straits that Mama Day "in her dreams ... finally meets Sapphira" [280], who is the female equivalent of Moses, who had powers that defied any simple explanation.

Mama Day has inherited many of Sapphira's gifts. It is fitting that she be a leader in the Candle Walk where the residents of Willow Springs have in the past chanted: "Lead on with light, Great Mother. Lead on with Light" [111]. All the marchers must bring with them some source of light (a kerosene lamp, a candle, or even just a sparkler) in reverence to the Woman who freed them. And the walk is not without practical value. Just as the Bible has as one of its admonitions that "it is more blessed to give than to receive" (Acts 20:35), those who participate in the Candle Walk must give something to someone else. The nature of the walk allows people in need to accept gifts without submitting to a condescending charity. Whether walk participants give a handful of cookies or a bushel of potatoes, "it all got accepted with the same grace, a lift of the candle and a parting whisper, 'Lead on with light'" [110]. Such altruism cannot be taught in religious seminaries. Nor can it be bargained for in that ongoing activity of tabulating who will receive eternal life for doing what deeds. Rather, the Candle Walk is a distinctly woman-inspired effort to achieve a morally legitimate community within which true godliness can thrive.

A Missing Brother:
The Ultimate Inadequacy
of the Reverend Jasper

In a 1992 interview, fellow author Quincy Troupe asked Terry McMillan, "What do you think that men have to learn?" Her response was, "They need to understand something about passion. . . . A lot of men don't have enough convictions about things" [52]. *Waiting to Exhale* (1992) provides several good examples of what McMillan means because in this novel she presents us with a wide variety of men who are lacking in dedication and are willing to abdicate crucial responsibilities. What these men have in common is the ability to live selfishly notwithstanding the fact that others are depending on them for emotional and financial sustenance.

But we can go back to McMillan's first novel, *Mama* (1987), to see this particular theme of male inadequacy played out to its fullest extent. In the small town of Point Haven, Michigan, Mildred (Mama) has suffered indignations varying from a public beating administered by her husband, Crook, to the day-to-day ordeal of having to raise and provide for their five children by herself. Mildred's oldest daughter, Freda (the alter ego of McMillan herself who was raised in Port Huron, Michigan), has very distinct feelings about what is going on:

She didn't like seeing her mama all patched up like this. As a matter of fact, Freda hoped that by her thirteenth birthday her daddy would be dead or divorced. She had started to hate him, couldn't understand why Mildred didn't just leave him. Then they all could go on welfare like everybody else seemed to be doing in Point Haven [10].

Mildred does indeed eventually divorce her husband and finds herself going on and off welfare, in between stints of menial employment, as she goes through the process of raising her children alone.

In *Labor of Love, Labor of Sorrow* (1985), author Jacqueline Jones has drawn certain conclusions about the interplay of black women, family, and work. She finds that "despite great difficulties in making ends meet, many mothers derived extraordinary pride and satisfaction from the well-being of their children, and they viewed life according to the options available to their offspring" [222]. This would explain how Mildred, a high school dropout, can nevertheless demand of her children, "Every last one of y'all is going to college" [27]. As McMillan tells us, "These kids were her future. They made her feel important and gave her a feeling of place, of movement, a sense of having come from somewhere" [13]. Mildred is the major reason why each of her children will find some degree of success in their lives.

McMillan is not unsympathetic with regard to the plight of black men in America, however. The time is 1964, and the author concedes, "Most of the black men couldn't find jobs, and as a result, they had so much spare time on their hands that when they were stone cold broke, bored with themselves, or pissed off about everything because life turned out to be such a disappointment, their dissatisfaction would burst open and their rage would explode" [19–20]. The artist there reveals the same concern that Haki Madhubuti expresses in his introductory comments to *Black Men: Obsolete, Single, Dangerous?* (1990) as he describes "young black men in their late twenties or early thirties living in urban America, lost and abandoned, aimlessly walking and hawking the streets with nothing behind their eyes but anger, confusion, disappointment and pain." And certainly, McMillan will reinvestigate this theme through the character of Franklin Swift, who at one point in *Disappearing Acts* (1989) bemoans the subway "full of black men who looked mad at the world" [110]. He himself fails to overcome the crippling self-perception that he is little more than a common day laborer.

One cannot help but believe, however, that Crook would be better off if he had even a modicum of the passion Mildred shows toward their children. True, he is only a sanitation worker. But Mildred has been at various times a maid, a waitress, a cook, a factory worker, or a caretaker for the elderly. What is the essential difference between Crook's occupation and the tasks Mildred has had to perform? The types of employment are in fact quite similar. Any difference has to do with how society demands prestige from men. Men are expected to perform more dignified labor that in some sense reflects who they are. If this is not possible, then it has an effect on their egos. They may even reach the point where they consider themselves less than "real" men. Such social perspectives are even more devastating for black men, who over the years have consistently received the worst of employment opportunities.

The detrimental impact of social attitudes was not lessened with the publication of Daniel Moynihan's 1965 report on the black family. He believed, as Michelle Wallace interprets the document, that "if you increase the black *man's* educational and employment opportunities – the implication was that you would ignore the black woman, who had too much already – you will increase the numbers of black status quo families with principal male providers and thus eliminate or substantially diminish the problems of blacks – in other words, unemployment, juvenile delinquency, illiteracy, fatherless households" [114]. Moynihan truly believed that the black community's major problem was that there were too many female-dominated households. But even as he criticized the overabundance of black matriarchs, he failed to acknowledge the danger of black patriarchy. Furthermore he took too much for granted in assuming that once black men had power it would as a direct consequence trickle down and filter into the overall black community.

Author bell hooks is enlightening as she renders the following assessment:

> Many black men who express the greatest hostility toward the white male power structure are often eager to gain access to that power. Their expressions of rage and anger are less a critique of the white male patriarchal social order and more a reaction against the fact that

they have not been allowed full participation in the power game. In the past, these black men have been most supportive of male subjugation of women. They hoped to gain public recognition of their "manhood" by demonstrating that they were the dominant figure in the black family [94].

The point that hooks makes here is especially important because she is in essence saying that from a black woman's perspective, it matters little whether the oppressor is a white male or a black male, her well-being will not be substantially altered. Many black men in pursuit of power have not been especially concerned about the very specific problems that black women face. Moreover, the circumstances of impoverished black children have not really been their priority.

Mildred's brother Jasper is one of these men with whom hooks finds fault. Early on in his life he was a frequenter of the local pool hall and was in fact shot for having stolen a beer. Now, however, he is a preacher with "so many kids he had to keep adding rooms onto his house so he could have somewhere to put them" [161]. One immediately notices the tone with which McMillan describes that housing necessity. He did not *want* to add rooms. He "had to." Not to be able to provide better shelter for them or raise them better or care for them. But "so he could have somewhere to put them." It might be argued that this particular phrasing is just indicative of McMillan's writing style. *Publishers Weekly* writer Wendy Smith observes that the author has a tendency to use "salty, often profane language." So it is conceivable that when McMillan says, "so he could have somewhere to put them," she indeed means "so he could have somewhere to love them."

I would submit, however, that McMillan means to say what she says in the particular manner that she says it. The author knows how to write so that it is clear when one person loves another. And this is not the sense we get from Jasper. Nor is it just his own children that he regards as objects. At one point in the novel when Doll and Angel, two of Mildred's daughters, have returned from California to visit yet another sister, Bootsey, they all "didn't want to go see him, because he'd never been very friendly" [161]. Again, some might wish to defend Jasper. We all, at one time or another, have seen images of the self-possessed, respectable minister, aloof from everyday happenstance. Such men are often regarded as being above the ordinary fray of what consumes so much of other people's lives. But to have an uncle who has *never* been friendly – and is a preacher – is something to which we must pay attention. Indeed we must wonder just how far he has come since those days when he might have been shot for stealing beer in a pool hall. What manner of thief is he now?

In her essay entitled "Black Women and the Church," Jacquelyn Grant contends that "if Black theology speaks of the Black community as if the special problems of Black women do not exist, it is no different from the white theology it claims to reject precisely because of its inability to take account of the existence of Black people" [146]. Grant's comment reminds us of what hooks has to say about the false distinction whether black women are being oppressed by white men or black men. hooks emphasizes the desire of black men to prove their manhood through the acquisition of economic power. What Grant does, in her essay, is explain how the black church has facilitated what have been the efforts of black men to participate in the patriarchy even to the detriment of black women.

Early on in *Mama*, we get a sense of where McMillan will lead us in terms of how black theology is promulgated by the religious leaders of Point Haven. There is much to consider in her story about another preacher who when he

> put on his white robe and walked through waves and over stones to baptize people, he wouldn't go out too far. Once he dropped his Bible in the water after dipping Melinda Pinkerton backward into salvation and a wave clipped his sleeve, sweeping his Bible away. He didn't try to go after it, either [28].

The preacher cannot be very far out in the water, but he will not bend down to retrieve an item so sacred as his own personal Bible. We can just envision this "apostle" jumping back from the wave as though at any second it might destroy him. "Forget God," he must be saying to himself. Forget the Bible. It is evident his faith is not genuine.

Although Mildred may appear on the surface to be one of the most irreverent characters in the annals of American literature, that presumed irreverence merits a close look. Curly, her sister-in-law, criticizes Crook for drinking too much, confiding to Mildred,

"Abusing hisself like he do ain't nowhere in the Bible, is it?" [42]. Mildred responds, "Honey, I wouldn't know, been so damn long since I read it" [42]. We could conclude that these are simply the words of an unabashed nonbeliever.

On another occasion, Freda asks Mildred why most black people are poor. Mildred answers, "They thank they can get something for nothing and that that God they keep praying to every Sunday is gon' rush down from the sky and save 'em" [27]. In that answer we can begin to understand that Mildred is not an atheist at all. She just has her own beliefs about how faith in God should be pursued. Although she is acquainted with the Bible, she is nevertheless not now an avid Bible reader. And she does not accept the notion that regular church attendance by itself is the means to earthly success or other worldly salvation.

Mildred has had such a rough life that her particular faith has to be structured around the cold, hard reality of her very practical existence. She has had to raise five kids alone, and then when it seems that she has pretty much accomplished this feat, her father has a heart attack. She is in California when her sister Georgia calls her with the details. The doctors do not know if he will survive, but Georgia cavalierly proclaims, "The Lord is watching over him" [234]. In another one of her seemingly irreverent responses, Mildred tells Georgia, "I'll be on the next plane out of here. My daddy need me more than he need the Lord" [235]. Mildred remembers how eager Georgia was to move in with their father when their stepmother died. It had been Georgia's intention to take advantage of their father's pension and the life insurance payments he would be receiving as a consequence of his wife's death. It was Mildred in that instance who had stopped Georgia dead in her tracks, threatening, "If I have to come back there and put padlocks on the doors myself, you ain't using my daddy" [202].

As already mentioned, Mildred is living in California. Another brother, Leon, resides in Arizona, so Georgia is free to take advantage of her father's circumstances. But where is the other brother, Jasper, who has been residing in Point Haven all along? Why is it that he can do nothing to prevent Georgia from exploiting their father? One can only fathom that this son does not care. In fact, Jasper can be said to have a great deal in common with Georgia, who has "turned her soul over" to God for the purpose of sheer convenience. Georgia tells the story of how her husband returned from the grave to get her to drive back and watch her house burn down. Not only will she get insurance money but also a chance to move in with her father. Similarly, Jasper has undergone a "conversion" that will allow him to take advantage of others' unfortunate circumstances. In spite of the widespread poverty suffered by blacks, he has positioned himself to acquire wealth. And we are left with the question of just how concerned he really is when it comes to the community for which he is presumed to be a spiritual steward.

Jasper is not available for his father in time of need, and certainly not for Mildred and her children as they negotiate a plethora of precarious events. His sister struggles through furnace breakdowns, utility cutoffs, and finally eviction, and never once do we see him appear and offer assistance. If nothing else, one would think he could show concern for Mildred's only son, Money. After that child has fallen prey to drug addiction and been incarcerated, the narrator contemplates a succession of causes that amounts quite simply to his having had to assume the responsibilities of manhood far too early in his adolescent development. In one of the more poignant sections of the novel, McMillan conveys:

> When Mildred and Crook split up Money had become the man of the house at eleven years old. It was Money who picked up the dead mice because everybody else was too scared. It was Money who drained the water from the basement when it flooded. Waded through three inches of water just to put the clothes in the dryer so the girls could wear matching knee socks to school. It was Money who learned how to put a penny in the meter to get the lights and gas back on when they'd been cut off. It was Money who pulled the trash barrels out to the street to be picked up. And when things broke, Money fixed them. No one had taught him; his instincts told him what to do. . . . They all took it for granted that this was his role. He had never had any options [122].

Money got his name because by the time "he was barely old enough to tell you his address" [46], he had become a beggar. He would ask, "You got a dime?" If the person he was asking said no, then Money would ask, "You got a nickel?" If the person still said no, then the child would implore, "Well you got *any* money?" Before long, this habit of begging became one of stealing, as a downward spiral continued.

But the main point is that while all this is going on, Jasper is nowhere to be found. In some ways he resembles Kristen Hunter's the Reverend Bird, for whom his congregation "contributed enough to the church collections to provide him with all the antiques ... he required for his happiness. And since *their* happiness required that their pastor be transported in a large, elegant car and the Reverend Bird did not drive, they could hardly object to his series of chauffeurs" [*Lakestown Rebellion*, 32]. We have seen in my earlier chapters how comfort and prosperity for the preacher can take priority over even the basic needs of church members. Bird does at least fight government officials when it seems that the interests of his congregation are in jeopardy. There is absolutely no evidence, however, that Jasper is inclined to project himself into the forefront in defense of the interests of those he would acknowledge as his flock.

Keep in mind that Jasper is for the most part an artistically effective preacher. He knows how to deliver a "fire and brimstone" sermon. As Curly confirms, "Jasper still preaching like ain't no tomorrow. The words be like music filling up your body" [245]. On the one occasion we see him elocuting, the congregation as a whole is awe-inspired, following along in the same "call-and-response" manner that characterizes black preaching at its best. The "Tell its," "Amens," and "Ain't that the truths" are a testament to the speaker's undeniable force.

Still, the sermon is problematic. It is useful here to consider another Jasper – the John Jacob Jasper who was my own grandmother's minister. This preacher is especially famous for having sought to convince his listeners that the sun revolved around the earth instead of vice versa. "De Sun do Move" was the title of that sermon he delivered over and over again from one Virginia church to another. In his talks he relied on Malachi 1:11, where it says, "For from the rising of the sun even unto the going down of the same my name *shall* be great among the Gentiles." But we immediately see the flaw in that Jasper's interpretation. Even today, televised weather reports include the times of sunrise and sunset. But this is not to say that those who use the terms believe that the earth is the center of the universe. Galileo proved the opposite four centuries ago.

John Jasper found it useful to proliferate a contradictory

theory of his own devising, however, and he was a gifted enough speaker to be utterly persuasive. One need only put himself in the position of an illiterate former slave to comprehend how easy it might have been to be swayed by the famous preacher's words:

> Has I proven my point? Oh, ye whose hearts is full of unbelief! Is you still holding out? I reckon de reason you say de sun don't move is cause you are so hard to move yourself. You is a real trial to me, but, never mind, I ain't given you up yet and never will. Truth is mighty; it can break de heart of stone and I must fire another arrow of truth out of de quiver of de Lord [230].

John Jasper spoke in brilliant metaphoric terms as he depicted himself shooting arrows from the Lord's quiver in order to pierce hearts that resisted his versions of the truth. As was the case with Hurston's John Pearson, and indeed all of the preachers we have covered in this study, the power of words can have a blinding effect that impedes the listener from realizing the deeper truths about humanity and the world.

McMillan's preacher is similarly fallible. Jasper, like his historical namesake, can enrapture an audience with wonderful metaphors, asking on one occasion, "Do it feel like you in a boat rowing backwards when the island you trying to get to is up ahead?" [176]. Jasper understands the psychology of this small factory town where "women usually did day work" and for more than a few, welfare checks were "steadier and went a lot further" [30] than what regular employment would provide. In fact, Freda, who has no idea where she will move, nevertheless cannot wait until the day when she will graduate from high school and leave this town because "she knew that there had to be a better place to live than here" [28]. Not everyone will be so single-minded as Freda is in their efforts to get out of Point Haven. But Jasper is aware of the deep-seated misery festering within the black population. "*Sometimes*," he exhorts his congregation, "you can get so full of sorrow and so heavy-hearted, that you feel like you in a jail run by Satan" [176]. He touches their emotions in a way that places special emphasis on the torment he knows is being suffered.

But why is it Jasper seems to give so little help in ameliorating the awful societal conditions? We will remember how Paule

Marshall has suggested that there is no difference between the preacher and the rum seller. Interestingly enough, McMillan raises the same issue when she notes that "drinking was the single most reliable source of entertainment for a lot of people in Point Haven. Alcohol was a genuine elixir, granting instant relief from the mundane existence that each and every one of them led" [19]. In addition to the many McMillan characters who possess a "salty" vocabulary, there are also quite a few who are hard drinkers, including Mildred. But such characters are meant to be admirable. They are survivors. And as they move from the church to the barroom, we witness a capacity to persevere, notwithstanding life's problems. There evidently are times when the obscurities and contradictions that are lodged in Jasper's words simply are not enough.

For example, Jasper tells the story of a teenage girl who, having injured her ear, "couldn't hear nothin' but a roaring sound" [177] for two solid years. Now Jasper is eager to get to the part where he talks about God completely restoring the girl's hearing. The preacher speaks of her unwavering faith and tells how she prayed persistently. In the story, the girl's hearing is restored. Yet anyone paying careful attention to the story's details would have to ask how someone who hears only a roaring noise can sleep "so very sound" over the course of the same two-year period. An all-powerful God could of course provide for a person to sleep peacefully through such a roaring sound, even if it is deafening. But considered from another perspective, it makes little sense. God will not answer her prayers for two years, but He allows her to be at peace with the roar, making her premiracle condition not all that drastic as the preacher would have us believe.

Jasper goes on to tell these "healing stories for what felt like hours to Mildred" [178]. The entire sermon has really become an ordeal for her as she eases the high-heeled shoes off her feet and dreams of being able to get even more comfortable and smoke a cigarette. "The power of Almighty God is *Swift. Immediate*" [178], says the preacher in his sermonic commentary on the girl with the ear problem. If taking two years to accomplish something could be called swift and immediate, then perhaps Mildred would be swayed by her brother's reasoning. Under the circumstances, however, she is not impressed.

Jasper says, "*desire* is prayer," and that "in order to find God, you must first have discernment" [177]. McMillan tells us that Mildred does not even know what that last word means. But this is not to say the author would have us believe that the hardworking mother is stupid or in some other way lacking in necessary intelligence. Mildred does not know what the literal definition of *discernment* is, and those of us who do know what the definition is find ourselves wondering what Jasper himself wants to convey in saying what amounts to "In order to find God, you must first have found God." Mildred's confusion is but a reflection of the confusion we should all have at hearing such a statement.

I will refrain from even attempting to interpret the reverend's statement that desire is prayer, other than to say that the lack of any information with regard to what is being desired makes a virtual plethora of possibilities exist for what prayer is being equated with. We are reminded of how John Jacob Jasper sought to convince his congregation that the sun revolved around the earth. That Jasper convinced numerous listeners he was correct. McMillan's preacher wants to have that same kind of oratorical power. In fact, he does have such power, for there are many who will do whatever he says and follow him anywhere. Mildred, on the other hand, is the type of person who never will be deterred from the scientific findings of Galileo.

Considering the methodology of John Jacob Jasper, it is very likely that he would have been unsuccessful in attempting to convert Mildred to Christianity. At the conclusion of her brother's sermon, she mulls over what he has said but is ultimately disappointed. The author tells us, "She did not feel an inch closer to God" [179]. Mildred needs the kind of hard, cold facts that are implicit when she admonishes her son, "Money, boy, where you thank that bike you ride all over town come from? God?" [73]. She knows first hand of the day-to-day strivings required if people like her are to achieve anything. In fact, a strong sense of inappropriateness is conveyed by the author as she has the main protagonist drop "one of her last five dollars into the brass plate" [178] when Jasper asks for donations. We cannot help but believe that it is he who should be contributing to her social betterment instead of the other way around.

It is not only because Jasper espouses himself to be a man of

God that we think he should be making some more tangible contribution to Mildred's life. We believe this because he is also her brother. But in a dramatic chapter near the end of the novel, we are confronted with a stark reality. Jasper will never be available for Mildred. In the scene where Mildred walks out into snow and zero-degree temperature to get to her sister-in-law who has been hospitalized for a stroke, this long-suffering woman is in dire need of some kind of support. When she first gets the news of Curly's illness, she "considered going to the hospital, but she felt so tired she sat back down in the chair by the window" [249]. Several hours pass before she attempts again, but "she hadn't had a drop of strength left in her" [249].

It would seem logical here for Mildred to phone her brother and ask if he could drive her to the hospital. Such duties fall under the rubric of pastoral responsibilities anyway. Since Curly is a member of Jasper's congregation, perhaps he has already visited her. If such is the case, then Mildred could simply call him to inquire about her best friend's condition. But she does not call. And we do not get the sense that Jasper has visited Curly at either the hospital or her home, where even Mildred "couldn't stand being . . . too long because it depressed her" with its "dark, rickety furniture" [40]. No, if anyone was going to be there for Curly, it would have to be Mildred. Support from the Reverend Jasper is tenuous at best.

Maybe Curly joined church for the wrong reasons anyway. Earlier she had poured out her troubles to Mildred:

> Shelly most likely gon' spend the rest of her life in and out of prison, Chunky half crazy from them drugs, and last night, chile, some boy beat Big Man in the nose with a poolstick and he up in Mercy Hospital right now. . . . My husband don't even touch me no more, Milly, so you turn to whoever gon' make you feel the most glory and peace. And for me, right this minute, it's God. If it weren't for him, I don't know if I'd even have the strength to get up in the morning and face daylight [245].

Curly for some time now has been mourning the circumstances of her immediate family. Her children are a disappointment, and she is unable even to receive solace from her husband. For her, God is a last resort, a crutch, a diversion from the reality which would otherwise drive her to despair.

After listening to Curly's explanation for why she joined the church, Mildred offers that friend her best wishes, saying, "Well, more power to you, Curly" [245]. But then when Curly asks Mildred to attend church with her the following Sunday, Mildred defers, maintaining, "Last time I went to church I got depressed" [245]. Curly presses further in the fashion of an evangelist herself, insisting, "That's 'cause you didn't give yourself a chance to let God in. Once you let him in, it feel so good . . . you won't want to turn back" [245]. "I'd love to sit here and chitchat with you all day," Mildred says, as she abruptly ends the conversation, "but I got thangs to do" [245].

Mildred is primarily a doer in spite of her limited resources. This is why later in the novel, after struggling against her own weariness, she is finally able to lift herself up out of the chair and go outside to the car she has borrowed from Bootsey. She is determined to get to the hospital. Relying on God is not enough. The author had told us at the beginning of the book that when it came to acquiring money, Mildred "didn't think he was such a reliable source" [31]. When it comes to looking out for her friends, Mildred is not willing to turn that mission over to God either.

Driving through the snow, Mildred skids and gets trapped in a snowbank, but she is not injured. In fact, she reserves most of her remorse for Curly rather than for herself or her immediate predicament. But it is during this incident that we see Mildred at her most introspective. One might even be inclined to say that she is praying as she talks out loud to some unknown entity:

> If you up there, I hope the hell you can hear me. I wanna know what the hell you trying to prove? . . . Why can't you do something right for a change? I thought you was supposed to be so big and bad, could do anything anytime anywhere. Are you there or am I just wasting my damn time? [250–51]

The language is sometimes profane as she asks whoever she is speaking to whether this is "some kind of damn test." She wavers back and forth between giving up (at one point she says, "I've had it") and being determined to overcome this adversity, proclaiming, "I'm gon' tell you something, buddy. I'm gon' make it past the finish line" [251]. In the final analysis, she will not give up, and in the process of this struggle, we are witness to the blossoming of a faith that is nothing like what occurs in the rarefied atmosphere of a church sanctuary.

Carlene Hatcher Polite, in *The Flagellants* (1967), presents us with a character named Ideal, who as a child witnesses the verbal power of the minister at her great-grandmother's church. The response of the congregation is identical to what the McMillan's Reverend Jasper is able to evoke from his parishioners. Polite's preacher is so effective that "brothers and sisters of the church whooped and hollered for release" [10]. Meanwhile, Ideal, sitting beside her great-grandmother, observes all the commotion and silently questions:

> Where was the God who had created the flowers, the light, the heart of this place called Black Bottom? Who was the God who had chosen our mothers to bring us into the world? Where was the God who is love? [11–12]

After thus contemplating, the child "cried tears of ignorance." This protagonist has legitimate questions about how the world is composed, particularly her segregated, less affluent side of town. That she is ignorant about the status of God should not be viewed as evidence of any flaw in her character. Remember that her name is "Ideal," and the questioning search that she is conducting may be meant to serve as a model for others who would seek to investigate the deeper meanings of life.

There are those who look at J.D. Salinger's *The Catcher in the Rye* (1951) and find in Holden Caulfield only the musings of a disturbed adolescent who can make neither heads nor tails of the world other than to condemn all adults for being phoney. Perhaps this young man is being overly sensitive. But perhaps the kind of analysis he is conducting is essential for an understanding of those things that many others have been willing to take for granted without any true understanding at all. He is not to be taken literally when he says, "I'm sort of an atheist" [99]. The operative phrase there is "sort of." How is someone sort of an atheist? An atheist does not believe in God or Jesus. Maybe agnostic would be a better word to describe Holden. But if he is agnostic, why does he go on to talk about Jesus as though he really existed? And he has harsh words for the disciples. "They were all right after Jesus was dead and all," contends Holden, "but while He was alive, they were about as much use to Him as a hole in the head" [99]. Blasphemy some might say. I, on the other hand, argue that this is the kind of straightforward analysis that both Ideal and Mildred are capable of conducting. Theirs is the methodology by which answers are obtained.

In the snow, Mildred gets out of the car to examine her situation. She immediately discovers that she has a flat tire, which was what caused her to skid. But she does not know how to change a car tire. It so happens that Jasper lives only a half mile down the road. But Mildred still has on her indoor shoes, and the author uses this fact as the reason why she cannot walk to his house for help. It is rather intriguing that Mildred has brought along her coat and gloves but somehow neglected to put on boots. In walking across the snow to the car at her house, it should have dawned on her that some type of outdoor footwear would be needed.

We should consider the precise language McMillan uses in depicting Mildred at her residence walking "across the hard snow" that "crunched under her house shoes" [249]. For indeed the snow may be so hard that it basically holds her weight, giving in, as the author tells us, only to a limited extent and then only under her shoes. Had snow been engulfing her feet at every step, it seems she would have noticed a need for boots. So if the snow was that hard right outside her house, why is it not just as hard on Fortieth Street where the car has run off the road? She would not have to trudge through wet snow to get to Jasper's house. She should be able to glide there just as easily as she had walked out to Bootsey's car in the first place.

The narrator posits the question thusly: "Why hadn't she put her snow boots on when she left? Jasper's house was damn near a half mile down the road" [251]. Considering that the word "damn" is used here, we can assume that this is how Mildred contemplates her situation. But rather than having Mildred's dilemma being a mere quirk of fate, the author is intentionally placing obstacles to prevent her from reaching her brother. And thereby the point is emphasized just how distant this brother is. He is in essence much more than just a half mile away. He is entirely unreachable. He was not available for Mildred's son. He was not available for his own father. And now while Mildred undergoes her ordeal out in the snow, his availability looms once again as a question.

The physical barriers between Mildred and her brother are not formidable. Even if the snow was wet and sloshy, she could have warmed her feet upon her arrival at his home. Moreover, she could have walked in the paths created by car tires in the middle of the road. But the author wants to convey that it was easier for Mildred to change the tire herself (something she had never done before) than receive any kind of satisfactory help from Jasper. One wonders how satisfactory is the help that he would give anyone.

During his sermon, Jasper urged the congregation to believe that "God is within you." It sounds like a revolutionary notion along the lines of what Shug, in *The Color Purple*, tells Celie. "God is inside you," Shug says, "and inside everybody else" [202]. Yet while Shug encourages self-identification and explains how the search for God should be conducted, Jasper succumbs to contradiction. God is inside people according to the preacher, but he also says, "*God* alone lessens the sum total of all evil" [178]. Jasper first joins God in a physical mutuality of responsibility and then separates Him based on sermonic convenience. His congregation apparently adheres to the message in spite of it being inherently flawed.

Mildred needs more than shallow words, especially at this point when Bootsey's car is hopelessly trapped in the snow. As if in direct response to this need, a communion takes place that is unlike anything she could have achieved in Jasper's church. Whereas at one point during her ordeal, she questioned God's existence, now she is talking to Him as though He will give concrete help. "Look," she beseeches, "it's a lot of thangs I could've done differently, I know that. And I ain't never asked you for much" [251]. There is remorse in those words, but she is not quite apologetic. Rather, she has accepted the circumstances of her life, asking little help from God until times arise when she absolutely needs it.

For Mildred, "*faith* in God alone" is not enough. In her case Jasper would have been well advised to draw from Thessalonians II, where Paul reminds the crowd that those who follow him do not "eat any man's bread for nought; but wrought with labour and travail night and day, that we might not be chargeable to any of you. . . . If any would not work, neither should he eat" (3:8 and

3:10). Mildred would have been able to identify with the substance of those passages. That mother went through torment when she was laid off from two housekeeping jobs she held simultaneously. As a consequence, she had to sign up for welfare. The author informs us that "this humiliated and embarrassed the hell out of her – Mildred hated the idea of begging, which is what she thought it boiled down to.... She had always prided herself on being self-sufficient and self-reliant" [34–35]. But with five children to support, she needed the assurance of a steady income. Pride would have to be sacrificed.

In verse 11, Paul criticizes those who "walk among you disorderly, working not at all, but are busybodies." Jasper seems not to be bothered so much by the large number of blacks in the community who are on welfare. Just as long as he gets a certain percentage of their income, whatever its source, he is satisfied. Mildred, however, has a different vision that ironically enough is more in line with Paul's teachings than anything Jasper has thus far offered. McMillan may well have drawn this aspect of Mildred's character from her own mother. In an interview with Molly Giles, McMillan recalls that her mother was

> one of the strongest women I've ever met in my life, and I think what I learned from her was how not to be afraid.... She taught us to test ourselves in every way. If I got a *B* on my report card in math, she'd say, "That's great; next time get an *A*." ... We never got any Happy Face stickers. But she made all five of us strive to outdo ourselves, always. She never finished high school herself.... She was a domestic and worked for a lot of rich white people [34].

The evidence is strong that Mildred is the alter ego of the author's own mother. Mildred has five children, just like McMillan's mother. In addition, the two mothers are high school dropouts who have had to work off and on as domestics. But neither mother wants our pity. They regard life as a test to be passed or failed in proportion with the amount of effort they have exerted.

So when Mildred goes on welfare, she must exert even more energy, now in the effort to get off the public dole. Toward this end, she garners all her inner resources and in the process of doing so, she refuses to go to church because she "didn't like the nosy people in town knowing all her damn business" [34]. How little has changed in the 2000 years since Paul delivered his message in Corinth. The "busybodies" that he spoke of are now the "nosy people" of McMillan's novel, who are, Mildred would have us believe, substantially to blame for the persistence of problems in the black community. Rather than contributing to the betterment of their social environment, they spread malicious gossip and thus make us want to examine their moral code.

In her volume of poetry entitled *Bronze* (1922), Georgia Douglas Johnson included a poem that embodies the spiritual self-analysis that Mildred will undergo a full 65 years after that poem was written. Even the poem's title reflects the vacillating tendencies that are sure to exist in the psyche of anyone who seriously ponders the extent to which God influences people.

MOODS

My heart is pregnant with a great despair
With much beholding of my people's care,
'Mid blinded prejudice and nurtured wrong,
Exhaling wantonly the days along:
I mark Faith's fragile craft of cheering light
Tossing imperiled on the sea of night,
And then, enanguished, comes my heart's low cry,
"God, God! I crave to learn the reason why!"
Again, in spirit loftily I soar
With winged vision through earth's outer door,
In such an hour, it is mine to see,
In frowning fortune smiling destiny! [32]

Within the first two lines of that poem is the concern for a race of people who have been much maligned. McMillan's mother inculcated in her children her belief that blacks should push themselves even harder to overcome that adversity. "She taught us," McMillan states in the Giles interview, "that we could be anything we wanted to be. And if we didn't believe it, then she was going to ram it down our throats until we did" [34]. One hears echoes of Paul addressing the Galatians, entreating them to "not be weary in well doing: for in due season we shall reap, if we faint not" [6:9]. Mildred has this understanding about life as she, like McMillan's mother, has accepted the value of hard work.

Mildred is capable of a certain callousness about the issue of faith. As she reflects on God early in the novel, we are told, "she didn't think he was such a reliable source" [31]. Yet we must consider the context within which she expresses that sentiment. A paragraph earlier in the novel, we were presented with the scene where women realized they would receive more money from welfare than from working a job. These particular women "spent their afternoons watching soap operas" [30]. Mildred, however, tries to keep working, knowing that for her, "nobody was coming by to drop off a bundle of dollar bills unless it was God" [31]. And this is when she calls God unreliable since she believes He will do no such thing.

Still, like the narrator in "Moods," Mildred is intrigued by the prospect of understanding the fiber of real faith. Of what does it consist? What is the nature of her responsibility in the bargain? In Johnson's poem, faith is personified, "Tossing imperiled on the sea of night." Therein lies a crucial question: Will faith survive? It is the same question Mildred subconsciously entertains during a thunderstorm when, while sitting on the sun porch with Spooky Cooper, she issues the maxim, "My daddy always saying a thunderstorm is the Lord doing his work and we should be quiet" [63]. While it is true that she says this because she is "unable to think of anything else to say" while she and Spooky are "listening to the thunder and the rain falling in the drain pipes" [62–63], it is significant that she even thinks of this. It is as though faith was lurking in her all along like a wellspring that was waiting to be tapped.

Although she had never changed a flat tire before, Mildred determinedly goes to the trunk, pulls out a jack and lug wrench, and proceeds to remove the flat tire and replace it with the spare. She has never asked much of God and now largely due to her own efforts, she accomplishes what she never imagined she could. She concludes, "Hell, this wasn't as hard as she thought it was" [251]. In Johnson's poem, the narrator evolves through her spiritual dilemma with the newfound power of a bird in majestic flight. "In spirit loftily I soar / With winged vision through earth's outer door," the poet writes. By the time she has completed the tire-changing job, Mildred likewise is filled with supernatural exhilaration, feeling "like she could probably fly if she flapped her arms fast enough" [251].

The car is still stuck in the snow, but we are not as worried as we were earlier when it first ran off the road. It has now become evident that a contract of sorts is in effect between Mildred and the God who has helped her throughout the years she raised all those children. Here in the middle of the night, after first trying to drive the car out of the snowbank and then unsuccessfully trying to push it out, she addresses God, imploring, "I'm gon' ask you to help me one last time, and I swear I'll do everythang else myself" [252]. Having uttered that request, she strains with all her might against the car, loses her balance, and falls in such a mysteriously awkward way as to cause the car to roll out of the snowbank with her lying prone on the hood. As the car glides loose, we are left in a quandary about which of the partners is most responsible for that success.

When Jasper is preaching, one woman in the congregation blurts out, "All I see is fog" [176]. Like Mildred and the speaker in the poem "Moods," she may be involved in intense spiritual self-analysis. Jasper's brusque response, rendered in midsermon, is, "It's the devil causing all that fog" [177]. But how can he be sure that the vagaries of life have not been caused by God pressing people to test their fortitude? McMillan, in the Giles interview, was concerned that "any time you give men power, they will abuse it" [37]. This theme is certainly apparent in the artist's other novels. In *Disappearing Acts*, Franklin exploits Zora's undying love. In *Waiting to Exhale*, the vast majority of men prey on women like hawks pursuing frantic field mice. One would assume that a reverend would be considerably better than the men who appear in those other two works. Instead, in Jasper we see yet another man misappropriating the devices available to him. This preacher does not have all the answers. Needless to say, no one human being does. But behind Jasper's high-sounding words lies a sordid mentality incapable of helping where help is needed most while he impedes the progress of those who come to God on their own.

Conclusion

It is apropos here to reconsider the significance of Naylor's offering us Mama Day as "God's" earthly agent. This elderly woman's motivations are purely altruistic, and it is therefore good to compare her to others (such as Father Peace) who are intent on establishing earthly kingdoms for themselves. As we all too well know, formalized religion has developed to the point where it often functions no differently from a profit-making business enterprise. Preachers are the major beneficiaries, and the people in the congregations are but the means whereby such men have acquired immense personal power.

The phenomenon is widespread but has especially profound implications in the African American community, where the church has historically been the most important and the most powerful institution. When greed and corruption have taken precedence over saving souls, there have been few other institutions to which African Americans could turn for support after disillusionment. Black "commoners" simply endured those imperfections or completely dropped out of the church scene. Such limited options are indicative of a tragedy that has persisted over countless generations.

I do not want to be misunderstood here. Within the context of the African American community, the black church has produced more leaders than any other type of organization. From Richard Allen in the 1790s to Nat Turner in the 1830s to Adam

145

Clayton Powell, Sr., in the 1920s and Jesse Jackson in the 1980s, black preachers have been at the vanguard of social change. Malcolm X and Martin Luther King, Jr., both ministers, were perhaps the greatest leaders black Americans have ever had. All of these men are part of a rich tradition that employed religion in engendering social progress.

A problem, however, arises when we try to understand how those leaders envisioned total fulfillment of their goals. In the process of fighting for social change, how much new freedom could the black woman expect? What new provisions were being fought for so that her previously limited options for self-actualization could be increased?

Alice Walker's Celie in *The Color Purple* imagines God as "big and old and tall and graybearded and white. He wear white robes and go barefooted" [201]. It is the vision of God rendered by Michelangelo during the early sixteenth century, as he painted his ceiling frescoes in the Sistine Chapel. A vision of God that, I would wager, most modern Christians have accepted as appropriate.

Pictures can have a powerful influence. As black boys worship such a God, we should be concerned about the resulting psychological consequences. It has been argued that the picture is just a symbol and we should all know that God really is a spirit; we are not certain what he looks like. But it is no mere accident that the symbol selected is an evidently all-wise white man. In many people's minds, the symbol can quickly turn into reality, and we wind up worshiping in a misguided fashion.

When the more worldly Shug Avery laughs at Celie's version of God, Celie, in something of a quandary, asks, "What you expect him to look like, Mr. _____?" [201]. Celie here offers what, for her, is the next logical choice. Mr. _____, of course, is black, but nevertheless a man, a particularly domineering one (abusive, in fact); and as far as Celie is concerned, he is a more viable candidate than any woman, black or white. The most severe tragedy is that she never would have envisioned God as looking like herself. Standards of male domination have seen to that. A black girl worshiping the white male version of God should also be of grave concern to us, for what we have in essence is someone worshiping what can be regarded as the exact opposite of herself. In such a situation, what are the chances for an emotionally healthy acquisition of identity? Father Peace appears to want social progress, but at what price to the individual? As is the case with many religious denominations, each individual Peace follower must be sacrificed for the organizational whole. Marshall and the other major writers considered in this text reject such processes as being too detrimental to the interests of women. If men are allowed such unfettered domination, then abuses of the system will take place. The sin of adultery will, in all likelihood, rage on. And even within the home, women will continue to find their husbands utilizing the Bible to perpetuate male oppression.

Marshall and Naylor would have us investigate a distant past for the positive aspects of African culture. As a result of this investigation, perhaps the image of God would better reflect who blacks in America actually are. Perhaps material acquisitions would no longer be a necessary element of religious practice. Mama Day is symbolic of such a movement away from Westernized versions of religion with their trappings of whiteness and wealth. Having once suffered due to New World religious practices, the black woman has now become the spiritual leader. Willow Springs has benefited, and instead of prestige and power, the major aspiration is an ever-abiding closeness to God.

Annotated Bibliography

Abernathy, Ralph. *And the Walls Came Tumbling Down*. New York: Harper, 1989.

Born in Alabama in 1926, this civil rights leader retraces the path that led him from a rural farming community to the forefront of the civil rights movement.

Achebe, Chinua. *Things Fall Apart*. 1958. New York: Fawcett, 1989.

In his first novel, Achebe details the gradual process whereby Europeans gained access to the African continent.

Andrews, Larry. "Black Sisterhood in Gloria Naylor's Novels." *CLA Journal* 33 (1989): 1–25.

An evaluation of the sisterhood theme in Naylor's first three novels. Andrews concludes that the author's vision becomes increasingly complex as she moves from one novel to the next. While sisterhood in *The Women of Brewster Place* is a bond protecting women from oppression, sisterhood in *Mama Day* is a celebratory condition that facilitates communion with the spiritual world.

Angelou, Maya. *I Know Why the Caged Bird Sings*. 1970. New York: Bantam, 1977.

In this first volume of her autobiographical series, Angelou recounts childhood experiences in Stamps, Arkansas, and St. Louis, Missouri. It is a quintessential bildungsroman in that she develops from a child with literally no voice and very little self-esteem to a teenager embarking on the workaday world.

Aptheker, Herbert. *American Negro Slave Revolts*. 1943. New York: International, 1974.

Whenever one thinks of slave revolts, the names Gabriel Prosser,

Nat Turner, and Denmark Vesey come to mind. Aptheker, however, dispels the myth that those rebellion leaders were anomalies. He cites numerous instances of insurgency ranging from the sabotage of tools to the killing of plantation owners.

Baker, Houston A. *Workings of the Spirit.* Chicago: University of Chicago Press, 1991.

A preeminent African American literature scholar turns his talents toward assessing the impact that black women writers have had on American culture.

Bastide, Roger. *African Civilizations in the New World.* 1967. London: Hurst, 1971.

Bastide argues that African cultural carryovers exist in the Americas. He describes African religions in great detail, compares African American and native American traditions, and examines the clash between Protestant and early African perspectives.

Baym, Nina. "Melodramas of Beset Manhood: How Theories of American Fiction Exclude Women Authors." *American Quarterly* 33 (1981): 123–39.

As late as 1977, the established American literary canon included no women writers. Even as women writers are gradually being included, they are, Baym maintains, still subjected to certain biases as a consequence of the domination that men continue to exercise in the field of literary criticism.

Beckles, Hilary. *A History of Barbados.* Cambridge: Cambridge University Press, 1990.

Beckles traces Barbados from its Amerindian origins to colonization and the subsequent struggle for independence.

Bender, Lauretta, and M.A. Spalding. "Behavior Problems in Children from the Homes of Followers of Father Divine." *Journal of Nervous and Mental Disease* 91 (1940): 460–72.

Based on case studies involving the children of Father Divine devotees, this essay exposes the detrimental impact that cult participation has on such children.

Bender, Lauretta, and Zuleika Yarrell. "Psychoses Among Followers of Father Divine." *Journal of Nervous and Mental Disease* 87 (1938): 418–49.

A study of eighteen individuals who were admitted to the Bellevue Psychopathic Hospital as a consequence of having belonged to Divine's Peace Mission Movement. Bender and Yarrell summarize the membership requirements of that organization and explain how the loss of personal freedom eventually caused psychological trauma.

Boaz, Ruth. "My Thirty Years with Father Divine." *Ebony* (May 1965): 88–90, 92, 94–96, 98.
Boaz offers a startling insider's view of the Peace Mission Movement.

Bone, Robert. *The Negro Novel in America.* New Haven: Yale University Press, 1958.
An overview of the African American novel from William Wells Brown's *Clotel* in 1853 to Ralph Ellison's *Invisible Man* in 1952.

Brown, Emily. *Patterns of Infidelity and Their Treatment.* New York: Brunner, 1991.
Using numerous case studies, Brown explores the causes of marital infidelity.

Burnham, Kenneth. *God Comes to America.* Boston: Lambeth, 1979.
A glowing account of the Peace Mission Movement, the text is particularly useful for its appendixes, which summarize the vast property holdings of the organization.

Carby, Hazel. *Reconstructing Womanhood.* 1987. New York: Oxford University Press, 1989.
Drawing on nineteenth-century activists such as Anna Julia Cooper, Fannie Barrier Williams, and Fannie Jackson Coppin, Carby outlines the origins of black feminist tradition.

Christian, Barbara. "Gloria Naylor's Geography." In *Reading Black, Reading Feminists,* edited by Henry Louis Gates, 348–73. New York: Meridian, 1990.
In creating her fictional communities, Naylor conveys the manner in which black women have been socially constricted.

Collier, Eugenia. "The Closing of the Circle: Movement from Division to Wholeness in Paule Marshall's Fiction." In *Black Women Writers (1950–1980),* edited by Mari Evans, 295–315. New York: Anchor, 1984.
Collier examines the significance of African and Barbadian influences in Marshall's fiction.

Cooper, Anna Julia. *A Voice from the South.* 1892. New York: Oxford University Press, 1988.
Born a slave in 1858, Cooper overcame that adversity and went on to obtain a Ph.D. from the University of Paris in 1925. This text is one of the earliest statements of the black feminist movement.

Dante. *The Inferno.* 1321. In *The Portable Dante,* edited by Paolo Milano, 3–187. New York: Penguin, 1979.
Dante's version of hell consists of ten descending circles. The most sinful individuals are located near the bottom of this realm, with the Devil himself inhabiting the lowest sphere.

Davis, Arthur P. *From the Dark Tower: Afro-American Writers, 1900–1960*. Washington, D.C.: Howard University Press, 1974.

Limiting the scope of his study to those he considers to be major African American writers, Davis designates 1900 to 1940 as the period of black literary awakening. He further specifies 1940 to 1960 as a period during which black writers sought identification with the American literary mainstream.

Davis, Thadious. "Nella Larsen's Harlem Aesthetic." In *The Harlem Renaissance: Revaluations*, edited by Amritjit Singh, William Shiver, and Stanley Brodwin, 245–56. New York: Garland, 1989.

Relying on letters that Larsen wrote to various Renaissance luminaries, Davis speculates about what motivated this writer to pursue literary endeavors. Born into a working-class immigrant family, Larsen saw writing as a means to achieve social prominence.

de Beauvoir, Simone. *The Second Sex*. 1949. New York: Vintage, 1974.

Born in Paris and educated at the Sorbonne, this social critic draws primarily from her French experiences to explain the ways society discriminates against women.

DeVeaux, Alexis. "Paule Marshall: In Celebration of Our Triumph." *Essence* (May 1980): 96, 98, 123–34.

DeVeaux charts Marshall's development from when she was a researcher for a magazine to the point she achieved prominence as a novelist. Excerpts from an interview with Marshall are included.

Divine, Father. Interview with "Miss C." 28 January 1951.

In this interview, Divine criticizes blacks who use skin-lightening creams and hair-straightening products.

Douglass, Frederick. *Narrative of the Life of Frederick Douglass*. 1945. New York: Signet, 1968.

An eminent U.S. statesman describes his experiences as a slave.

Dove, Rita. Foreword to *Jonah's Gourd Vine*, by Zora Neale Hurston. 1934. New York: Perennial, 1990.

Dove points out ambiguities surrounding the main protagonist, John Pearson, and questions whether he is totally to blame for his actions. Although he is an adulterer, the community in many ways facilitates his immoral activity.

Du Bois, W.E.B. *The Souls of Black Folk*. 1903. Greenwich: Fawcett, 1961.

Du Bois makes many observations about African American culture. He opposes the educational policies of Booker T. Washington and declares that black Americans suffer from a state of double-consciousness.

Dunbar, Paul Laurence. *The Complete Poems of Paul Laurence Dunbar*. New York: Dodd, 1948.

A compilation of almost four hundred poems about blacks both during and shortly after the era of slavery.

Eliot, T.S. "The Hollow Men." 1925. In *T.S. Eliot: Selected Poems*, 75–80. New York: Harcourt, 1964.

This poem is but one example of Eliot's disillusionment over the moral decay he associated with the advent of industrialization.

Ellison, Ralph. *Invisible Man*. 1952. New York: Vintage, 1972.

A young black man wins a scholarship to college and thereby begins a process of personal development that leads him to New York City, where he learns about the complex motivations of people.

Emecheta, Buchi. *The Joys of Motherhood*. 1979. New York: Braziller, 1990.

Nigeria's most prolific woman novelist weaves a tale that reveals much about that country's cultural history. The title of the novel is ironic since the main protagonist, Nnu Ego, experiences great suffering as a consequence of having to rear nine children.

Faulkner, William. *Absalom, Absalom!* 1936. New York: Vintage, 1972.

The story of Charles Sutpen, who is intent on starting a family dynasty but learns that he destroyed that possibility when he deserted his first wife and failed to acknowledge his black son.

_____. *Light in August*. 1932. New York: Vintage, 1972.

Faulkner tells the story of Joe Christmas, a man who suffers in Christ-like proportion as a consequence of being neither black nor white in a world that demands he be one race or the other.

Fauset, Arthur Huff. *Black Gods of the Metropolis: Negro Religious Cults of the Urban North*. Philadelphia: University of Pennsylvania Press, 1944.

An overview of religious cults that certain types of blacks have been inclined to join.

Fleming, Robert. "The Influence of *Main Street* on Nella Larsen's *Quicksand*." *Modern Fiction Studies* 31 (1985): 547–53.

Fleming draws parallels between *Quicksand* and *Main Street*. The major character in both novels is a woman who attends college and gets married, only to discover that her actions will be severely restricted because of her gender.

France, Anatole. "The Procurator of Judea." In *Mother of Pearl*. London: Lane, 1908.

Years after the crucifixion, France's fictional version of Pontius Pilate cannot even recall Jesus' name.

Fuller, Hoyt. Introduction to *Passing*, by Nella Larsen. 1929. New York: Collier, 1971.

Fuller connects the main protagonist, Clare Kendry, to the author herself as he accuses them both of rejecting their blackness.

Gavins, Raymond. *The Perils and Prospects of Southern Black Leadership: Gordon Blaine Hancock, 1884–1970*. Durham: Duke University Press, 1977.

Hancock was the pastor of Moore Street Baptist Church in Richmond, Virginia, from 1925 through 1963. He was, in addition, a race relations expert who published widely and lectured at dozens of colleges and universities.

Genovese, Eugene. "Black Plantation Preachers in the Slave South." *Louisiana Studies* 11 (1972): 188–214.

In the midst of precarious circumstances, the slave preacher found ways to inspire the dream for freedom while yet appearing to support the status quo.

_____. *Roll, Jordan, Roll*. New York: Pantheon, 1974.

Taking for his book's title the words of an old slave song, Genovese depicts the world of slavery as rich in culture in spite of the accompanying evils of that peculiar institution.

Gloster, Hugh. *Negro Voices in American Fiction*. Chapel Hill: University of North Carolina Press, 1948.

Gloster analyzes black fiction in terms of various phases that include pre–World War I, the Harlem Renaissance, and the era of the Great Depression.

Grant, Jacquelyn. "Black Women and the Church." In *All the Women Are White, All the Blacks Are Men, but Some of Us Are Brave*, edited by Gloria T. Hull, Patricia Bell Scott, and Barbara Smith, 141–52. New York: Feminist, 1982.

Historically, black women have been the backbone of the black church in terms of their roles as support workers. Nevertheless, there has been a reluctance on the part of men to share leadership positions.

Hacker, Andrew. *Two Nations*. New York: Scribner's, 1992.

A political scientist analyzes extensive data and arrives at the conclusion that America remains a nation that is essentially divided by race.

Hackett, George, et al. "A Sex Scandal Breaks Over Jimmy Swaggart." *Newsweek*, 29 February 1988, 30–31.

America's most prominent televangelist is discovered to have been committing adultery with a prostitute.

Harris, Trudier. "No Outlet for the Blues: Silla Boyce's Plight in *Brown Girl, Brownstones*." *Callaloo* 6 (1983).

Harris examines how the Barbadian immigrant Silla Boyce has been driven by capitalistic impulses since her arrival in America. Although Boyce understands the plight of those who are locked in the underprivileged classes, she is not above exploiting them for economic gain.

Hatcher, William E. *John Jasper: The Unmatched Negro Philosopher and Preacher.* New York: Revell, 1908.

Hatcher details the sermons and other public presentations that made Jasper as much a folkloric phenomenon as he was a devoted clergyman carrying out the functions of his office.

Hawthorne, Nathaniel. "Young Goodman Brown." 1835. In *Norton Anthology of American Literature*, 1st ed., vol. 1, edited by Ronald Gottesman, et al., 910–21. New York: Norton, 1979.

In this allegorical tale about the nature of evil, a young man leaves home and ventures into the forest, where he discovers all the townspeople communing with the Devil.

Hemenway, Robert. "Are You a Flying Lark or a Setting Dove?" In *Afro-American Literature: The Reconstruction of Instruction*, edited by Dexter Fisher and Robert Stepto. New York: Modern Language Association, 1979.

Borrowing a courtship ritual expression from one of Zora Neale Hurston's novels, Hemenway proceeds to argue that much of African American poetic performance has its origin in African culture.

———. *Zora Neale Hurston: A Literary Biography.* 1977. Urbana: University of Illinois Press, 1980.

The definitive Hurston biography, this work as much as anything else aided in the revival of Hurston as a major American author.

Herzog, William. "The 'Household Duties' Passages." *Foundations* 24 (1981): 204–15.

There is a tendency among some feminists to discount the Bible as not being an adequate guide for modern male/female relationships. Herzog contends, however, that certain passages from Colossians and Ephesians should be interpreted in terms of a mutuality of responsibility between men and women.

Hill, Adelaide. Introduction to *Quicksand*, by Nella Larsen. 1928. New York: Collier, 1971.

Pointing out the importance of novels written by black women, Hill nevertheless uses *Quicksand* to argue that Larsen was confused about her own racial identity.

hooks, bell. *Ain't I a Woman: Black Women and Feminism.* 1981. Boston: South End, 1984.

hooks assesses the status of black women in American society. She evaluates the ways that white women have been put on a pedestal and examines how black women's struggles have been different from those of white women.

Hostetler, Ann. "The Aesthetics of Race and Gender in Nella Larsen's *Quicksand.*" *Publications of the Modern Language Association* 105 (1990): 35–46.
Hostetler maintains that the most vivid images of female suffocation occur in this novel when Helga Crane is forced to view herself through the confining social constructs of gender and race.

Howard, Lillie P. *Zora Neale Hurston.* Boston: Twayne, 1980.
This literary biography is an important contribution in the effort to revive fully an essential black author.

Huggins, Nathan. *Harlem Renaissance.* 1971. New York: Oxford University Press, 1974.
The first full-scale treatment of the Harlem Renaissance.

Hughes, Langston. *Mulatto.* 1935. In *Five Plays by Langston Hughes,* edited by Webster Smalley, 1–35. Bloomington: Indiana University Press, 1973.
A prototypical tragic mulatto tale. Hughes's protagonist demands treatment in accordance with what is given white men. His demands, however, meet with a tragic conclusion.

Hunter, Kristin. *The Lakestown Rebellion.* New York: Scribner's, 1978.
An all-black community resists the implementation of a highway construction project that will severely disrupt the neighborhood.

Hurston, Zora Neale. *Dust Tracks on a Road.* Philadelphia: Lippincott, 1942.
Winner of the *Saturday Review*'s Anisfield-Wolf Award for having contributed to the betterment of race relations, this autobiography has nevertheless been criticized for rendering too shallow an analysis of the author's life.

_____. *Jonah's Gourd Vine.* 1934. New York: Perennial, 1990.
Based to a large extent on the lives of Hurston's parents, the novel examines marriage, infidelity, and the operations of the black rural church.

_____. *Moses, Man of the Mountain.* 1939. New York: Perennial, 1991.
Hurston combines folklore, fiction, and comedy as she offers an alternative reading of the biblical Moses.

_____. *Mules and Men.* 1935. Bloomington: Indiana University Press, 1978.
The first extensive collection of black folklore to be compiled by a black American and published by a major book company.

———. *The Sanctified Church*. Berkeley: Turtle, 1981.
This text consists of essays written by Hurston during the years between 1926 and 1943. Her aim was to define and preserve the rich heritage of Southern black religious practices.

———. *Seraph on the Suwanee*. 1948. New York: Perennial, 1991.
In a unique turn of events, Hurston portrays a Southern white family. As with her depictions of blacks, Hurston remains concerned about the obstacles that prevent women from developing themselves.

———. *Tell My Horse*. 1938. New York: Perennial, 1990.
The result of Hurston's travels to Jamaica and Haiti, this book is further evidence of the author's folklore-collecting skills.

———. *Their Eyes Were Watching God*. 1937. Urbana: University of Illinois Press, 1978.
Hurston's masterful investigation of whether marriage is detrimental to female self-discovery.

Jacobs, Harriet. *Incidents in the Life of a Slave Girl*. 1861. New York: Harvest, 1973.
A young slave fends off her master's sexual advances and escapes to the North, where she records how especially difficult slavery was for a woman.

Jasper, John. "De Sun Do Move." In *The Book of Negro Folklore*, edited by Langston Hughes and Arna Bontemps, 225–33. 1958. New York: Dodd, 1983.
Jasper's famous sermon in which he asserts that the sun revolves around the earth. He uses Malachi 1:11, notwithstanding that this biblical passage refers to sunrise in the figurative sense.

Johnson, Georgia Douglas. *Bronze: A Book of Verse*. Boston: Brimmer, 1922.
The second of four books of poetry published by Johnson, this volume focuses on the difficulty of being black in America. These verses cover the gamut from utter despair to a hopefulness in terms of possible solutions.

Johnson, James Weldon. *The Autobiography of an Ex-Coloured Man*. 1912. New York: Hill, 1981.
The nameless narrator is of mixed parental heritage and consequently must struggle to ascertain what should be his racial identity.

———. Preface to *God's Trombones*. 1927. New York: Viking, 1983.
Johnson proclaims that many of the old-time black preachers were absolute geniuses. Explaining why he did not use black dialect for these seven sermons in verse, he says he wanted to avoid the limitations of a stereotypical language.

Jones, Jacqueline. *Labor of Love, Labor of Sorrow: Black Women, Work, and the Family from Slavery to the Present.* New York: Basic, 1985.
Informal female leadership customs have existed in many black communities. Only in recent years, however, have these women begun to gain real control over the products of their labor.

Kapai, Leela. "Dominant Themes and Technique in Paule Marshall's Fiction." *CLA Journal* 16 (1972): 49–59.
Kapai notes some rather obvious themes functioning in the fiction of Marshall, such as her use of the bildungsroman motif. The critic then proceeds, however, to specify more intriguing features such as the artist's preoccupation with the subconscious of her characters and her tendency to portray mothers in a negative light.

Larsen, Nella. "Freedom." 1926. In *An Intimation of Things Distant: The Collected Fiction of Nella Larsen,* edited by Charles Larson, 11–18. New York: Anchor, 1992.
The author examines the psyche of a man who proceeds to gain freedom by deserting the soon-to-be mother of his child.

———. *Quicksand.* 1928. In *An Intimation of Things Distant: The Collected Fiction of Nella Larsen,* edited by Charles Larson, 29–162. New York: Anchor, 1992.
Tormented by her mixed ancestry, Helga Crane journeys from one region of the country to another and even overseas in the attempt to discover her proper place in the world.

———. "The Wrong Man." 1926. In *An Intimation of Things Distant: The Collected Fiction of Nella Larsen,* edited by Charles Larson, 1–9. New York: Anchor, 1992.
Julia Hammond encounters a man she recognizes as Ralph Tyler, whose mistress she was in the past. When she asks him not to discuss their prior liaison with her husband, Tyler responds by seeming not to even know who she is.

Larson, Charles. Introduction to *An Intimation of Things Distant: The Collected Fiction of Nella Larsen,* edited by Charles Larson. New York: Anchor, 1992.
Larson dispels many of the negative myths surrounding Nella Larsen. He furthermore reserves her rightful place beside such notables as Toni Morrison and Zora Neale Hurston.

Lewis, Sinclair. *Main Street.* 1920. New York: Signet, 1980.
Carol Kennicott graduates from college only to discover that there are many limitations on what women can do in a male-dominated world.

McDowell, Deborah. "'That Nameless . . . Shameful Impulse': Sexuality in Nella Larsen's *Quicksand* and *Passing.*" In *Black Feminist Criti-*

cism and Critical Theory, edited by Joe Weixlmann and Houston A. Baker, 139–67. Greenwood, Fla.: Penkevill, 1988.

McDowell speculates about the concerns Larsen must have had as she examined black female sexuality in an era heavily influenced by Victorian mores. Larsen had to contend with the reality that at that time sex for a woman was considered shameful unless sanctioned by a marriage contract.

McKay, Claude. *Banana Bottom.* 1933. Chatham, N.J.: Chatham, 1970.

Bita Plant, the main protagonist, must choose between British culture and those Afrocentric elements of her Jamaican heritage.

McKay, Nellie. "Remembering Anita Hill and Clarence Thomas: What Really Happened When One Black Woman Spoke Out." In *Race-ing Justice, En-gendering Power,* edited by Toni Morrison, 269–89. New York: Pantheon, 1992.

When Hill sat before the Senate Judiciary Committee and accused Thomas of sexual harassment, she violated a long-standing taboo that black women should never openly criticize black men. McKay evaluates that taboo as well as other unique features of the Clarence Thomas confirmation hearings.

McMillan, Terry. "A Conversation with Terry McMillan." Interview with Quincy Troupe. *Emerge* (October 1992): 51–52, 56.

McMillan reveals aspects of her artistic development. She talks about her work schedule and specifies which authors influenced her style.

———. *Disappearing Acts.* 1989. New York: Washington Square, 1990.

In this novel the question is raised whether a financially secure woman should pursue a relationship with someone whose employment is limited in terms of prestige and income.

———. Interview with Molly Giles. *Poets and Writers Magazine* (November/December 1992): 32–43.

McMillan talks about her mother, college life, and her work experiences in a foreclosure department.

———. *Mama.* New York: Washington Square, 1987.

This novel recounts the trials and tribulations of a black woman relying on survival instincts in the process of raising five children.

———. *Waiting to Exhale.* New York: Viking, 1992.

The story of four black women who support one another through a series of stressful situations.

Madhubuti, Haki. *Black Men: Obsolete, Single, Dangerous?* 1990. Chicago: Third World, 1991.

Madhubuti examines the extent to which black men may be an

endangered species. Upon considering issues such as illiteracy, AIDS, and intraracial miscommunication, the author further points out that the black race as a whole is endangered.

Marshall, Paule. *Brown Girl, Brownstones.* 1959. New York: Feminist, 1981.

The story of Selina Boyce, a first-generation American who must reconcile the differences between her hard-working, ambitious mother and her easy-going, idealistic father.

_____. *The Chosen Place, the Timeless People.* 1969. New York: Vintage, 1984.

Set on a Caribbean island, this novel involves a clash between the forces of industrialization and those who seek a simpler, more spiritual lifestyle.

_____. *Daughters.* New York: Atheneum, 1991.

A novel explaining how blacks are often placed in high positions to facilitate the status quo instead of to improve the conditions of the masses.

_____. "From the Poets in the Kitchen." In *Reena and Other Stories,* 1–12. New York: Feminist, 1983.

In this autobiographical essay, Marshall acknowledges as the greatest source of her storytelling abilities those maids who would go to work and then return to converse in the basement kitchen of her mother's house.

_____. *Praisesong for the Widow.* New York: Plume, 1983.

Avey Johnson is a middle-class, middle-aged black woman who once believed that the quest for material possessions was a laudable pursuit. But she learns that the ultimate meaning of her life is tied to her Caribbean and African heritages.

Masters, William, Virginia Johnson, and Robert Kolodny. *Human Sexuality.* 4th ed. New York: HarperCollins, 1992.

These experts on human sexuality explore the physiological, psychological, and social implications of a vast assortment of sex-related issues.

Morrison, Toni. *Beloved.* 1987. New York: Plume, 1988.

Examining the ultimate depths of love, Morrison has an escaped slave woman kill her own child to save it from the horrors of slavery.

_____. *Song of Solomon.* 1977. New York: Signet, 1978.

Milkman Dead investigates his cultural roots and learns, among other things, that some of his African ancestors could literally fly.

Moynihan, Daniel P. "The Negro Family: The Case for National Action." Washington, D.C.: U.S. Department of Labor, 1965.

This study is most famous for its position on the issue of black matriarchies. Moynihan concludes that female headed households have been a limiting factor in the overall progress of blacks.

Naylor, Gloria. *Linden Hills*. 1985. New York: Penguin, 1986.
Using Dante's *Inferno* as a model, Naylor renders her own version of hell as an earthly domain where souls are exchanged for material prosperity.

_____. *Mama Day*. New York: Ticknor, 1988.
Located off the coast of Georgia, Willow Springs is an island whose residents resist the onslaught of industrialization.

_____. *The Women of Brewster Place*. 1982. New York: Penguin, 1983.
Women living in a housing project struggle for some semblance of dignity.

Naylor, Gloria, and Toni Morrison. "A Conversation." *Southern Review* 21 (1985): 567–93.
Two prominent black women authors discuss the recent proliferation of black women writers.

Pemberton, Gayle. "A Sentimental Journey: James Baldwin and the Thomas-Hill Hearings." In *Race-ing Justice, En-gendering Power*, edited by Toni Morrison, 172–99. New York: Pantheon, 1992.
Pemberton draws on a statement Baldwin made in 1961 with regard to black men being perceived as phallic symbols. Baldwin further asserted that even white liberals had difficulty recognizing the humanity in blacks. Accordingly, argues Pemberton, many who viewed the Thomas-Hill hearings had difficulty moving beyond certain racial stereotypes as they analyzed the sexual harassment charge.

Petry, Ann. *The Street*. 1946. Boston: Beacon, 1985.
The story of a young black woman who becomes locked into inner-city poverty. She immediately falls prey to various men who perceive her as a readily accessible sex object.

Polite, Carlene Hatcher. *The Flagellants*. 1966. Boston: Beacon, 1987.
A young black man and woman fall in love with one another, only to be victimized by the social demand that they conform to specific gender roles.

Pratt, Annis, et al. *Archetypal Patterns in Women's Fiction*. Bloomington: Indiana University Press, 1981.
Focusing on the works of established women writers as well as writers who are less recognized, Pratt discerns patterns in the ways all the authors handle issues such as marriage, social protest, and solitude.

Rich, Adrienne. "Disloyal to Civilization." In *On Lies, Secrets, and Silence*, 275–310. New York: Norton, 1979.

Rich analyzes the ways in which women have been relegated to an inferior status. She argues against tokenism and insists that what is needed instead is a sweeping transformation of human relationships.

Sakenfeld, Katharine. "Feminist Uses of Biblical Materials." In *Feminist Interpretation of the Bible*, edited by Letty Russell, 55–64. Philadelphia: Westminster, 1985.

Conceding the temptation on the part of feminists to reject Christian dogma, Sakenfeld nevertheless finds biblical passages to counteract verses often used to rationalize female subservience.

Salinger, J.D. *The Catcher in the Rye*. 1951. New York: Bantam, 1964.

Holden Caulfield, the main protagonist, is disturbed by what he perceives as phoniness in adults. A question arises whether his feelings are typical of adolescent behavior or proof that he is maladjusted.

Sheffey, Ruthe T. "Zora Neale Hurston's *Moses, Man of the Mountain*: A Fictionalized Manifesto on the Imperatives of Black Leadership." *CLA Journal* 29 (1985): 206–20.

Emphasizing the significance of Moses in African, West Indian, and African American culture, Sheffey asserts that Hurston uses him to challenge all who claim to be leaders of black people.

Smith, Wendy. "Terry McMillan." *Publishers Weekly*, 11 May 1992, 50–51.

Smith comments on the nature of the relationship between McMillan and her publisher and considers McMillan's insistence on using language styles that reflect modes of communication within the black community.

Stember, Charles. *Sexual Racism*. New York: Elsevier, 1976.

Stember explains how racism is to a large extent comprised of sexual attitudes that extend the barriers between blacks and whites.

Thornton, Hortense. "Sexism as Quagmire: Nella Larsen's *Quicksand*." *CLA Journal* 16 (1973): 285–301.

Early literary critics maintained that Helga Crane is tragic due to her inability to identify with either the black or white race. Thornton, on the other hand, emphasizes repressed sexuality as Crane's primary dilemma.

Turner, Darwin T. *In a Minor Chord*. Carbondale: Southern Illinois University Press, 1971.

Turner portrays Zora Neale Hurston, Countee Cullen, and Jean Toomer as talented writers who nevertheless failed to live up to their artistic potential.

Walker, Alice. *The Color Purple*. 1982. New York: Pocket, 1985.

This epistolary novel catapulted Walker into the forefront of

African American literature. The main character, Celie, is victimized by her husband in ways that are reminiscent of Janie Crawford's ordeal in Hurston's *Their Eyes Were Watching God.*

———. "Coming Apart." 1980. In *You Can't Keep a Good Woman Down,* 41–53. San Diego: Harvest, 1981.

Originally published in *Ms.* magazine under the title "When Women Confront Porn at Home," Walker compares contemporary views about women to the treatment black women received during slavery.

———. "If the Present Looks Like the Past, What Does the Future Look Like?" 1982. In *In Search of Our Mothers' Gardens,* 290–312. San Diego: Harvest, 1983.

In this essay originally published in *Essence* magazine under the title "Embracing the Dark and the Light," Walker voices concern about how the black race remains color conscious.

———. "Saving the Life That Is Your Own." 1976. In *In Search of Our Mothers' Gardens,* 3–14. San Diego: Harvest, 1983.

An essay proclaiming the importance of literary models. Walker mentions Zora Hurston as one of her personal favorites.

Wallace, Michelle. *Black Macho and the Myth of the Superwoman.* New York: Dial, 1979.

Wallace outlines the detrimental effects of two myths, one concerning the black male as a sexual animal and the other concerning the perception that black women can absorb endless abuse.

Ward, Catherine. "Gloria Naylor's *Linden Hills:* A Modern *Inferno.*" *Contemporary Literature* 28 (1987): 67–81.

Ward details the manner in which Naylor uses *The Inferno* to portray the moral decline of a black middle-class community.

Washington, Joseph R. *Black Sects and Cults.* New York: Doubleday, 1972.

This noted authority on African American religion traces the black religious experience from its roots in Africa through various adaptations undergone as a consequence of Christian influence.

Washington, Mary Helen. Introduction to *A Voice from the South,* by Anna Julia Cooper. 1892. New York: Oxford University Press, 1988.

Many intriguing details about the life of black feminist writer, Anna Julia Cooper.

Weisbrot, Robert. *Father Divine and the Struggle for Racial Equality.* Urbana: University of Illinois Press, 1983.

An extensive account of Father Divine's Peace Mission Movement. Weisbrot recreates the social climate that led up to the emergence of this prominent cult leader.

Welter, Barbara. *Dimity Convictions: The American Woman in the Nineteenth Century.* Athens: Ohio University Press, 1976.
Welter documents nineteenth-century perspectives on the roles of women in society. A dominant view was that women should be pious, submissive, and "pure." The author concludes, however, with a study of Margaret Fuller, who espoused feminist values in the midst of the nineteenth-century chauvinistic culture.

Wideman, John Edgar. *Brothers and Keepers.* 1984. New York: Penguin, 1985.
The story of two brothers raised by the same parents in Pittsburgh, Pennsylvania. One brother becomes a Rhodes scholar. The other is in prison, serving a life sentence for murder.

Willis, Susan. *Specifying: Black Women Writing the American Experience.* Madison: University of Wisconsin Press, 1987.
Willis analyzes the works of five specific black women writers to show how they use "specifying," a traditionally African American type of communication that consists of playful name-calling.

Wilson, August. *Fences.* 1986. New York: Plume, 1987.
Troy Maxson is unable to reconcile himself to the fact that he came along at a time when blacks were not allowed to play major league baseball.

Wright, Richard. *Black Boy.* 1945. New York: Perennial, 1966.
This noted author recounts his childhood days growing up in rural Mississippi.

Index